Prince Wen Hui's Cook

Chinese Dietary Therapy

by
Bob Flaws
and
Honora Lee Wolfe

Paradigm Publications   **Brookline, Massachusetts**

Prince Wen Hui's Cook
by
Bob Flaws and Honora Lee Wolfe

Library of Congress Cataloging in Publication Data
Flaws, Bob, 1946—
    Prince Wen Hui's Cook

    Bibliography: p.
    Includes index
    1. Diet therapy. 2. Medicine, Chinese.
I. Wolfe, Honora Lee, 1948—   . II. Title
RM216.F58   615.8'54   85—3398
ISBN 0—912111—05—4

Published by
Paradigm Publications
44 Linden Street, Brookline, Massachusetts

Cover Design by Herb Rich III

Table of Contents

Recipes

In Alphabetical Order

Dedicated to the Memory of

David Wilson, MD

A man who lived and died by Principle

Preface

In Chuang-Tzu's *Inner Chapters* there is a story about Prince Wen Hui and his cook. The cook gives the Prince a lesson on the Tao through the metaphor of cutting meat. As the wise cook says, after a period of time "practicing," one may reach a point where they "no longer see the cow" but "work with { their } spirit, not with { their } eyes { or intellect }. At that point the practitioner begins to spontaneously "follow the natural grain... taking advantage of what is there."[1] Thus, since dietary therapy is based on the same cosmological principles as all of the other Eight Limbs of Classical Oriental Medicine and spiritual science, through careful and insightful practice of such dietary therapy both as a therapist and as a patient, one may learn internally many of the "secrets of growth" as Chuang-Tzu calls them. The possibility of that growth has, in part, inspired the compilation of this work. *Bon Appetit*.

1

Introduction

Diet is the third of the Eight Limbs of Classical Chinese Medicine.[2] Although acupuncture and herbal therapy are much more widely known and popular in the West, if they are not supported by proper dietary therapy their effects will not be satisfactory or long-lasting. Chinese dietary therapy is based on the same cosmological principles as the other seven limbs. In particular, information on dietary therapy in the medical classics is largely found in the same sources as contain information on herbology. In fact, the difference between diet and herbalism is more a matter of the quantity of the food ingested than one of essential quality. In modern Chinese hospitals specializing in Traditional Chinese Medicine, dietary and herbal therapy are simply referred to as Internal Medicine.

This book is for practitioners and patients. Western practitioners of acupuncture and Chinese herbalism may not know or take into account Chinese dietary therapy and therefore fail to treat their patients both holistically and successfully. For patients, understanding diet can help provide a fuller comprehension of the philosophic and cosmological world view that is the foundation of Chinese medicine. It allows them to become more active and responsible participants in their therapy and will help to prevent imbalance before it arises.

In the health food marketplace the consumer is bombarded with all sorts of diets, additives, and supplements. Almost without exception these are recommended and used on a purely symptomatic basis: such-and-such a food is "good for" diarrhea. Yet no differential diagnosis of symptoms or discrimination of the different types of diarrhea is offered that would allow the individual to decide if a particular food would be therapeutic for *their* diarrhea. Chinese dietary therapy provides a detailed and clinically proven method of deciding if a given food is appropriate for any individual's personal condition. Such a theory of dietary therapy is therefore like Manjusri's Sword of Wisdom; it can quickly cut through a welter of conflicting opinions and ideas to arrive at an efficacious and personalized solution.

As American practitioners of Classical Chinese Medicine, my wife and I have attempted to translate Oriental principles of eating into contemporary, delicious, and nutritious American cuisine without undue dependence on, or fascination with, exotic Eastern ingredients.

The lietmotifs of Oriental life-arts in general are naturalness, unpretentiousness, and adaptability. It is inappropriate then to suggest that we Americans should eat Chinese, Japanese or Korean foods as our staples. On the other hand, because we are moving towards a global and more universal culture, "foreign" foods and ingredients have been suggested where appropriate. Humanity is the pinnacle of the natural world in part because we can and do eat so widely. We are able to assimilate, adapt to, and work with such a range of stimuli and environments because we eat omnivorously. Unfortunately the linear and dualistic sense inherent in the word "because" is not quite right. To be able to experience and *incorporate* as much as possible without prejudice is one of the goals of human life and our diet should reflect this.[3]

As in the other seven limbs, diet therapy is divided into three levels: Yogic or Alchemical, Preventive, and Remedial. Although in this book we have commented on the first two aspects of Oriental dietary therapy, our emphasis is on how to help a sick person become well through dietary management.

Yogic Diet

The foundation of all Oriental life-arts is the three principles of *Non-ego, Naturalness*, and *Non-doing. Non-ego* means the radical understanding that there is no independent, unchanging, or permanent self apart from everything else in the universe. According to Buddhist philosophy, all suffering, including disease, springs from our failure to understand and act upon this truth. We are ignorant of our fundamental non-existence and therefore we are attached to what we think will bolster our continued existence. We reject whatever we think may jeopardize that existence. Thus ignorance begets desire and repulsion, which in turn generate the 84,000 negative mental states that are on an ultimate level the cause of the 84,000 disease states. Due to this existential *hubris* we fail to act naturally. Instead of listening to the demands of the larger flow of the universe we seek our own separate peace. We go against the grain and act artificially. Once we start moving against the flow we must work even harder in this unnatural way. We become obsessed with doing and are terrified of letting things be, lest our own welfare not be promoted. Non-ego, Naturalness, and Non-doing do not arise nor are they obscured sequentially. Their manifestation or lack of manifestation is simultaneous.

The purpose of human life is to understand our own and everything else's non-ego and thus live naturally by non-doing. As the Lord Buddha taught, there is a technique or Path by which one can realize this. What one eats can play a part in the treading of this Path. This level of diet is called the Yogic or Alchemical level. It is comprised of very "unusual" dietary regimens based on millenia of yogic experience and experimentation. It is not for the average person nor even for the average Seeker. It is for the "professionally" religious or totally dedicated yogin working under the direct guidance of a Teacher who is both capable of transmitting the living lineage of such practices and who has mastered them through personal practice.

The Sanskrit word for this type of yogic diet is *Rasayana* and in Tibetan this is translated as *Chu-len* or "Alchemy." The basic idea is to gradually give up eating material food while progressively eating more and more ethereal food. This is done in controlled stages coordinated with meditation, yogic exercise, *and strict disciplines.* The ingestion of inorganic substances such as mercury is a part of this regime. Eventually the yogi or yogini is capable of living solely on Qi or Prana.

That is, he or she has become a Breatharian. This is called in Tibetan *Nam-kha Chu-len* or Sky Alchemy.[4] Extreme longevity may be a by-product of this type of practice but the ultimate aim is to achieve the *Ja-lu Pho-wa Chen-po* or Rainbow Body in which the physical body is dissolved into Clear Light leaving only hair and fingernails behind. The bodies of yogis who have practiced these disciplines but who have not achieved this sublimity are still transmuted in such a way that often their bodies do not decay after death. This is sometimes erroneously referred to as self-mummification. Attainment of the Rainbow Body is the perfect expression of Non-ego, Naturalness, and Non-doing.[5]

Short of attaining the Rainbow Body we are all diseased. However, this is from the ultimate point of view, not from the conventional, relative, or proximal point of view. Attempts by individuals to practice some part of this progressive Alchemical diet without the proper preliminaries, guidance, and supporting disciplines will only lead to further imbalance and disease. In my own clinical practice I see many young men and women who have been vegetarians for ten or more years for a mixture of spiritual, nutritional, and cultural reasons. Many of these patients now show signs of Deficiency of Qi and/or Blood due to this extreme diet. Vegetarianism is a step in the Yogic dietary progression. However, amongst mid-twentieth century Americans living in a temperate climate who have been brought up on high protein and animal product diets, it is questionable whether strict vegetarianism is healthy without a disciplined and active spiritual practice to supply a higher source of Qi.

From a spiritual perspective, whether one is practicing the esoteric levels of *Rasayana* or is following a more exoteric Path, the preparation and eating of food should be regarded as a sacrament. In Buddhism, preparation and ingestion of food can be viewed as a spiritual practice from several perspectives. From the Hinayana point of view it is a practice in Mindfulness, of being awake or aware in everything one does and every moment of the day. In Mahayana, one eats to sustain the body in order to work for the welfare of all sentient beings. In Vajrayana one can, by skillfully transforming the food into *Amrit*, the Nectar of Enlightenment, make every meal a Vajra Feast for the 100 Peaceful and Wrathful Dieties. Preparing and eating food on any of these three levels becomes a Dharmic practice, a source of Merit, and a positive force for the good of the world. Such a practice should be received from a lineal Teacher to validate and empower it.

5

Like every other aspect of our phenomenal reality, food is affected by how we think about it. Therefore the quality of the food is affected by the thoughts, mood, and motivation of the preparer. Anyone who has baked bread, brewed beer or grown a garden knows how living foods are affected by the mind-set of their creator. Food should be prepared with mindfulness, respect, precision, and gratitude. For this reason, often only highly trained and evolved monks were assigned as cooks in Chinese and Japanese Zen monasteries. From this point of view one's spiritual state directly affects the quality of the food which then affects one's health for better or worse.

Preventive Diet

From a mundane point of view we all want to live a long and healthy life. According to Chinese medicine, health and longevity are a product of our inherent constitution or inherited vigor and our moment to moment interaction with the universe. The more harmoniously we can live with the patterns of change in the universe the healthier we will be. To use the analogy of a stream, life will carry us like a boat rather than exhaust us as we try to swim upstream against the current. Generations of Sages through several recorded millenia have endeavored to understand the fundamental principles of change inherent in the universe. Oriental dietary theory and therapy is based on these principles as a means of preventing disease and maximizing longevity.

There are a certain number of principles that have pragmatic value in helping us align with the flow of life. We can understand phenomenal existence from the dynamics of any number from one to six. Each number stands for a principle that can help us comprehend and manipulate our existence. One equals absolute unity. Two is Yin/Yang. Three stands for the Three Powers of Heaven, Humanity, and Earth. Four represents the Four Phases of Change: Birth, Growth, Maturity, and Decline to death. Five represents the Five Elements and Six represents the Six Qi or Energies. In terms of Chinese cosmology, Five and Six are most often met when doubled, as in the Ten Stems and Twelve Branches. Each of these cosmological principles can be and is applied to Oriental dietary therapy. The first five of these six play a particularly important part in understanding diet as a preventive therapy. The sixth is more important for the remedial use of diet.

Non-Duality

From the point of view of One, Absolute Unity or Non-duality, everything that happens is appropriate. There is nothing out of place or undeserved. In terms of diet this means that one should live in the moment and not be overconcerned with the principles and rules of eating. If, while at someone's house, the universe serves up something out of season or not quite "right" in flavor or energy, one should not be too fussy or finicky. Rules and principles are only guides and are not substitutes for embracing and dancing with the moment. This relates to the fact that what we eat is not as important as what we think and what we do.

Yin and Yang

Yin and Yang, the two, are represented in the human body by Water and Fire. Contrary to popular Macrobiotic doctrine, Classical Chinese Medicine does not classify all food in Yin and Yang categories that can be laid out and linearly compared. As we will see in the section on the remedial use of food, each food is made up of a complex of Yin and Yang factors. A given food may be Yang in terms of flavor but Yin in terms of temperature or direction. From the classical point of view, Yin and Yang polarity is primarily useful in helping us avoid extremes of all kinds.

In preventive dietary therapy it is important not to eat too much. Overeating clogs the system with incompletely digested food and liquid or Glairy Mucous. This buildup of substance, or Yin, will impede the flow of Qi and Blood which will in turn impair the function, or Yang, of the organs. The eventual result of overeating will be depletion and Deficiency. Overeating not only harms the digestive system but also causes problems of circulation. Hemorrhoids, hypertension, and even tumors and boils may be caused by habitual overeating.[6] On the other hand if one eats too little one will not produce Qi and Blood sufficient to nourish (Yin) the function (Yang) of the organs. This also causes depletion and Deficiency. Whether Deficiency is caused by over — or under — eating, the result is Stagnation of Qi and Blood and eventual Collapse or death.

Another relevant Yin/Yang dichotomy is the temperature, both physical and energetic, of the food consumed. Food and drink should neither be too hot nor too cold. Food that is too Hot will damage the digestive organs, the structure or Yin. Food that is too Cold will put out the Middle Burner Fire or Yang. Also, too much liquid should not be consumed when eating. Liquid, Yin in nature, can also put out the Middle Burner Fire causing poor digestion and subsequent depletion of Qi and Blood. There is already a great deal of liquid in almost all food, even seemingly dry food such as bread. Also, since the Fire of the Kidneys is the root Fire of the entire organism it is important not to "drown" the Kidney Fire with too much water. The Kidneys are not just a sieve and are not really "flushed" by drinking copious amounts of water. The function of the Kidneys (Yang), an active transport system, is weakened by having to process too much water (Yin). This will eventually lead to polyuria, nocturia, and other signs of Kidney Deficiency. In clinical practice, the lack of Middle Burner and/or Kidney Fire is often seen among raw food and water-cleansing enthusiasts. Water intake should be balanced with urination. Chinese medicine considers normal urination to be three to four times per day in men and two to three times per day in women. Nocturia, arising from sleep at night in order to urinate, is abnormal and is an early warning sign of Kidney weakness.

Yin and Yang, Water and Fire, can also represent the balance between nutrition and elimination. There must be a balance between anabolism and catabolism, between building new tissue and replenishing vital energies and breaking down and eliminating toxins and wastes. There are many westerners who feel that toxemia or the presence of waste products and pollutants is the sole cause of disease. For such believers health care and disease prevention are simply a matter of cleansing through fasting, enemas, and colonics, or eating very eliminating foods such as fruits and raw vegetables, which are considered "Cooling" in Chinese medicine. From the Oriental point of view, toxemia is not the sole cause of disease. Disease and ill health are caused by hypofunctioning of the internal organs, hyperfunctioning of the internal organs due to attenuation of the physical substrate, and invasion of the organism by External pathogenic factors due to poor resistance. Each of these three etiologies may be caused by lack of nutritious, tonifying foods which are usually considered Warming, such as cooked vegetables, grains and small amounts of animal food. In general, patients who have over-emphasized fasting and cleansing present Deficiency syndromes characterized by a lack of warmth or Fire.

Cleansing or eliminating and nourishing or accumulating must be balanced. There is a time for each which is also based on Yin and Yang. Fall and Winter are the times for storing and tonifying; Spring and Summer are the times for eliminating. In preventive diet this is very important, since failure to follow seasonal commands of nature may not manifest as disease until subsequent seasons. Eating eliminating foods in the Spring and Summer when the weather is warm will not cool the system to the point where it will lack the Warm Defense Qi necessary to resist External invasion. Also, since the energy is moving up and out in the Yang seasons of the year and the body opens up to the environment naturally, the act of eliminating will require less energy to accomplish and will meet with less resistance on all levels.

In the *Nei Jing* it states that one should tonify Yin in Winter and tonify Yang in Summer. Traditional doctors have interpreted this dictum to mean that Cold and Cool foods and *herbs* should be eaten in Winter and Warm and Hot foods should be eaten in Summer. This seems to be a contradiction to the general principles of nourishing and eliminating. How can this apparent contradiction be resolved? I believe there are two ways.

First, Yin and Yang mean more than just Cold and Hot. Yin and Yang refer also to deep and superficial, rest and activity, lower and upper, nourishing and eliminating. In the Winter it is appropriate to eat foods that will move the energy down and to the core, that will tonify the roots (the Middle Burner and the Kidneys), and that will regenerate Essence and repair substance. In the Summer it is appropriate to eat foods that move the energy up and to the surface, that support increased activity and increased elimination, such as perspiration, and that make the Qi and Blood circulate freely and vigorously.

Secondly, this dictum is an injunction for us to think ahead. If we eat too much cooling food in the Summer it will weaken an already weak Yang energy at the core. All the Yang energy is at the surface leaving the core relatively more Yin. If we overindulge in cool foods we will harm the fragile Fire within. If great demands, such as copious perspiration which uses up Yang energy, create too much of a draw on this foundation Yang, its quality will be further diminished. Such is the case with summertime loose stools which come from eating too much fruit and salad. Likewise, in Winter, the Yin is stronger at the periphery than at the core. If we eat all warming and hot foods in Winter, we will overstimulate and attenuate and thus weaken the Yin. Some cool and cold foods should be eaten to offset this occurrence.

In traditional cultures, seasonal diet is instinctual. Christmas dinner is well suited to the energetic needs of Winter, just as a Fourth of July picnic is attuned to the needs of Summer. The apparent contradiction that Cold food is necessary in Winter is a reminder to nurture the Yin within Yang and vice-versa. It does not mean that we should violate common sense and custom. Apple pie and cranberry sauce complement turkey, turnips, potatoes, stuffing, carrots, and gravy. They are not the main course, only the condiments to keep everything in check.

In preventive dietary therapy, as in all life-arts, moderation is the key. The principle of Yin/Yang is one way to turn that key. Because it is seemingly simple to understand and apply, it is tempting to relate to it simplistically or rigidly. But, as the fictional Lama in *Lost Horizons* suggests, one should practice everything in moderation, even moderation. Life is dynamic and it is change. One should not use the Yin/Yang theory to try to attain some kind of *static* balance as a refuge from life, as some food faddists have done under the guise of this principle. To live humanely means to embrace, as Zorba the Greek put it, "the full catastrophe."

Qi, Blood, and Liquid

Representing Heaven, Humanity, and Earth, three simultaneously symbolizes Qi, Blood, and Liquid on the essential level of human physiology and Jing, Qi, and Shen on the quintessential level. To see the body only as a dynamic balance between function and substance is simple, but too general to allow for specificity of action. Each step from one to six is a movement towards complexity, but it is a complexity that enables us to interact with the flow of life with increasing precision.

Homeostasis in Chinese medicine is maintenance of the relative balance and proper functioning of Qi, Blood, and Body Fluids or Liquid. If any of these become excessive it will impair one or both of the others. Various foods affect each of these three "humours" differently. Some foods tonify Qi, others tonify Blood. Some foods tonify both Qi and Blood. Some foods produce Fluids; other foods reduce Fluid. Some foods control Rebellious Qi, decongest Stagnant Qi, and facilitate the flow of Qi. Similarly, some foods control, decongest, and facilitate the flow of Blood. However the balance of Qi, Blood, and Liquid is dependent upon the three "treasures" of Jing (Essence), Qi, and Shen (Spirit).

Jing, Qi, and Shen are the basis of the energetic physiology of the organism. They are the foundation of the Triple Heater as well as a symbol of the Triple Heater. Triple Heater Energetics have been described in English in several places.[7] However, in terms of diet, Jing refers to the Prenatal Essence or Kidney energy and Qi refers to the Middle Burner (Stomach/Spleen). Shen refers to the Spirit, Mind or psycho-emotional aspect of human incarnation. There must be a

11

reciprocal relation between the foundation Fire from the Kidneys (Ming Men, Ministerial Fire) and the Middle Burner or Postnatal Fire. Foods that maintain the Middle Burner Fire will indirectly benefit both the Spirit and the Essence. If the Middle Burner Fire becomes weak it will draw on the Lower Burner or Primordial Fire. This "Little Fire" supports the "Big Fire" or Mind.[8] If the Essence becomes depleted the Heart/Mind will become agitated and disordered. This in turn will further impair the digestive functioning leading to a vicious circle of depletion. Therefore, the Qi or Middle Burner Fire is called the Root of Postnatal Life. It is the pivot for Essence and Shen.

Preventively it is therefore of utmost importance to maintain the vigor of the Middle Burner Fire and this is done mostly through diet. Digestion is an oxidation process that requires heat. Food can be both energetically warm and physically warm from cooking. It is beneficial to eat primarily cooked foods and a proportionally greater quantity of energetically warming foods so as not to impair the digestive Fire. Food should be well chewed to make the work of the digestive Fire easier. It should not be eaten to excess or this will clog the "furnace" with "sludge," or Glairy Mucous. Not too much liquid should be drunk along with meals; it will smother the Fire and cause Water toxin. Iced and frozen foods should only be eaten sparingly and rarely. They are very detrimental to the Middle Burner.

The "heat" in food is dependent upon its Qi or vitality. Food that is stale, adulterated, processed, or left-over, is called "wrecked." Its essence is gone. Although it is physically present, it lacks the Fire of Life that supports the Stomach Qi. Food that has been cooked should be eaten within twenty-four hours. Left-overs should not be refrigerated since refrigerating and reheating destroys more of the vital essence of the food. It is a common experience that left-over and reheated food does not have its fresh bouquet and aroma. The purest essence of the food is in its smell and the loss of aroma is an indication that the food is wrecked. Likewise food should be organically grown, freshly picked or foraged, and as free as possible from toxins such as preservatives, insecticides, heavy metals, and pollutants. However, certain cultured foods such as miso, yogurt, and sauerkraut should not be considered wrecked since they are alive even though stored for long periods of time.

Four Phases

The four phases of change can be explained *vis-a-vis* preventive diet from two perspectives. One way to apply this principle is to divide human life into four ages: infancy, adolescence, maturity, and old age. Each of these four phases is marked by certain energetic peculiarities that require dietary adjustment. An infant is immature energetically. The Middle Burner is particularly sensitive and the Triple Heater as a whole is not very strong. Because the Middle Qi is not strong and stable the child is all too likely to produce Phlegm. This Phlegm will result in colds, runny noses, earaches, and general respiratory problems. Infants should not be fed too much meat and grain since their digestive Fire may not completely metabolize these foods, which would result in mucous production. Fruits and raw foods may only depress the Middle Qi further, resulting in loose stools. If the stools are chronically loose and if hard to digest food such as meat and grain is eaten, this will cause Infantile Phlegm. Easy to digest, warming foods such as cooked vegetables, a modicum of well-cooked grains (cream of wheat or rice, etc.), and only a little meat or meat broth should be the main staples of an infant.

Adolescents need large amounts of food to grow and build their adult bodies. The Fire of sex (Kidney Fire) flares and all too often may cause the Stomach Fire to also rise through the principle of draft. If the youngster consumes large amounts of greasy and spicy foods this heat rising from the Stomach may be exacerbated. If in addition there is simply too much food being consumed, Glairy or Hot Mucous may be produced. This scenario can cause everything from acne to emotional instability and hot-headedness. Therefore adolescents should be allowed to eat as their appetites dictate but they should be admonished not to eat too much excessively rich, fatty, or spicy food. Dietary imbalances during adolescence all too often cause disease in middle age.

During maturity one should eat widely, avoiding any tendency to eat a only limited range of foods. This will help one from becoming unbalanced by going to extremes. The full range of energies are necessary for health and the diet should be diverse. At the same time, too many different foods should not be eaten in the same meal. Once again, moderation is the key. Food should be eaten in a relaxed way. One should not eat when not hungry and one should not overeat. It is important to remember that we eat to live, not live to eat, so undue attention should not be placed on the diet either out of gluttony or purism and fastidiousness. Diet is important in maintaining health but one's mind-set and spiritual, psycho-emotional balance is more important. Undue rigidity concerning food is itself a disease-producing behavior.

During old age the Kidney Fire declines and the Yin is consumed. As the Kidney Fire becomes exhausted the Middle Burner Fire also becomes weak. Although one is at the other end of the spectrum the diet should revert towards that of the infant. Hard to digest and excessively cooling foods should be avoided. Amounts of food should be regulated and the Middle Qi should be carefully husbanded. The Middle Qi can indirectly nurture and support the Kidney Fire. Its abuse can also help to extinguish the Kidney Fire and with it, extinguish life.

On a smaller scale the four phases can help regulate one's diet through the four seasons of the year. In the Spring the energy moves up; in the Summer the energy moves out; in the Fall the energy moves down; and in the Winter the energy moves in. There are foods that can support each of these movements. Green, sprouting, above ground vegetables have an energy that moves up. Spices, flowers and leaves tend to have "floating" or outwardly moving energies. Root vegetables tend to have downward moving energy. Grains, seeds, and nuts have an inward moving energy. Foods should be eaten in season. Traditional methods of preservation usually correspond to the seasonal movements. Salting and souring both tend to bring the energy into the core.

Five Elements

Both within the microcosm of the body and the macrocosm of the external universe, five represents the Five Elements. Five Element Theory categorizes all of relative reality in five divisions. Each division is assigned to an "Element" and these elements interact according to certain predictable pathways. Each of the five flavors is assigned to an element. Likewise, each element governs certain body organs, tissues, senses, secretions, and even mental and spiritual states. There is then a relationship between the flavor assigned to an element and the organ and tissues assigned to that element. Five Element Theory, like the preceding principles, is used to promote homeostasis within the individual as that individual relates and reacts with the larger universe. Likewise, moderation is the keynote of Five Element Theory. Although a certain food or flavor may be nominally good for an organ in small or moderate amounts, too much of the same food or flavor will harm or deplete that same organ.

Many western practitioners have extrapolated from the Five Element Theory dietary practices and approaches that are not grounded in the two thousand years of Oriental clinical practice that is available. Most of the Five Element correspondences found in the medical literature are contained in the *Nei Jing* and *Nan Jing*. Those correspondences are scattered throughout numerous chapters. Westerners have tended to collect all these correspondences into one chart for ease of presentation. However, in so doing they often overlook the logic of the original presentation. Other westerners without access to the source materials are then apt to further compound this fallacious extrapolation. For example, the sour flavor belongs to the Wood element. Spring is also ruled by Wood. This does not mean, however, that sour food should be eaten in the Spring. Wheat is also related to Wood but nowhere in the classics or in Oriental clinical practice is wheat prescribed for the Spring. Although this approach looks good on paper and seems reasonable, it is both simplistic and erroneous. This literal use of Five Element correspondence panders to our insecurity and desire to be protected from the capriciousness of life by rigid rules.

In the *Nei Jing*, statements concerning the Five Elements and food are quite specific. In Chapter 23 of the *Su Wen* it says:

> "Travels of five flavors: sour travels to the Liver, pungent travels to the Lungs, bitter travels to the Heart, salt travels to the Kidneys, sweet travels to the Spleen, and these are called the five entering routes."[9]

In Chapter 78 of the *Ling Shu* it says:

> "Five travels: sour travels to the tendons, pungent travels to the Qi, bitter travels to the Blood, salt travels to the bones, sweet travels to the flesh. Such are called the five travels."[10]

There is no mention of eating flavors according to the annual Five Element seasons. In preventive dietary therapy, Five Element Theory primarily helps us avoid eating any of the flavors to excess by showing the consequences if we should overindulge. According to the classics,

> "If too much salt is eaten, the pulse will be sluggish and the complexion will lose its vitality. Too much bitter will cause the skin to dry and the hair to fall. Too much sour and the Liver will produce too much saliva which in turn will stifle the function of the Spleen. Too much salt and the bones will become weak, the muscles and flesh will wither and the functions of the Heart will be suppressed. If sweet exceeds the other tastes, the function of the Heart will cause difficult breathing and chest distention, a black color will appear, and the Kidneys will become imbalanced. If bitter exceeds the other tastes, the function of the Spleen will not be able to transfer fluids and the function of the Stomach will be too tense. If spice exceeds the other tastes, then the muscles and pulse will become slack and the Spirit will be injured."[11]

Five Element correspondences with meats, grains, and vegetables can be important in erecting a treatment plan once an imbalance has manifested. But for general purposes the theory is best used preventively as a reminder to eat widely and diversely without going to extremes.

Six Qi

Although six is an important number in terms of the numerological principles of Chinese cosmology, it does not correspond to any theories of diet on a preventive level of which I am aware. It is used to discuss the therapeutic or remedial actions of the six flavors. Six plays an important role in acupuncture, herbalism, astrology and geomancy *vis-a-vis* the Six Qi, the Six Stages of Cold Disease, the Six Energetic Layers of the meridian system, and as six doubled in the twelve Terrestrial Branches, twelve meridians, twelve months and twelve hours.[12]

Principles are conceptual aids to ordering our experience which allow us to make pragmatic changes based on our experience of reality. They are mind-made and are not real except on a relative and conceptual level. Principles should never distance us from lived life. They are tools and each has its own use. There is a saying that to a person armed with only a hammer everything looks like a nail. There is a time and a place to use each principle. Otherwise, we become abused by our principles, theories, and ideas.

Even the ideas of health and longevity should not be taken as absolutes. Throughout this section we have been discussing how to eat to avoid disease and attain longevity. Short of attaining the Rainbow Body, we all must eventually die. It is only a matter of time. We should not become attached to health and longevity, since ultimately they will fail us. But for those "on the Path" longevity and freedom from disease allow the opportunity to practice so as to transcend all notions of life and death, health and disease, pleasure and pain, good and bad. Otherwise, the pursuit of long life and health becomes itself a source of more attachment which is an inherently disease-producing process.

Remedial Diet

Chinese dietary therapy describes the medical qualities of foods exactly as Chinese medicine describes the qualities of herbs. There is a very fine line between herbs and foods. This line is particularly obscured when herbal liqueurs and soups are prescribed instead of pills, powders and decotions. The medical quality of each food is described from several points of view. It is only after all the various categories are taken into account that one can understand the nature of any given food. Each food is described according to its temperature, taste, meridian route(s), generalized direction in the body, Yin/Yang balance, Five Element ascription, therapeutic principles of action, specific symptomatic actions, common clinical use, and contraindications. These ten categories provide a comprehensive understanding of the energetic nature of a food and thus its commonly accepted clinical prescription.

Such detailed descriptions are what allow the physician to pass judgement with precision on the inclusion or exclusion of any food in any given patient's diet. Creating a dietary prescription then is no different from creating an herbal prescription. First the doctor must diagnose the patient using a combination of the four diagnostic modalities: inspection, listening/smelling, questioning, and palpation. The diagnosis may be couched in the terminology of organ or meridian syndromes (such as Liver Yang Excess or Cold Wet Obstruction of the Hand Yang Ming meridian); or in the terminology of Eight Principle syndromes (such as External Cold Excess); or in the Humoral descriptive syndromes (such as Up-flushing Qi and Water Toxin). From such a diagnosis the correct treatment principle can be easily inferred. For example, for a Liver Yang Excess the treatment principles are to sedate the Liver and to lower the Yang Excess. Once such a principle has been established it is logical that foods with complementary nature are beneficial or therapeutic and that foods of an antithetical nature would be harmful and exacerbate the pathology.

Within the overall picture, each descriptive energetic category has its own meaning and use. Depending upon the situation, a food may be beneficial for a patient in terms of one category but harmful in terms of another. All categories must be taken into account in determining the suitability or unsuitability of any food. Reliance on only one category, such as Yin/Yang balance or Five Elements, is a dangerous oversimplification even if the model has been correctly applied.

The basic methodology of Chinese medicine is heteropathy. A treatment is selected which will balance or cancel an imbalance or syndrome. Excesses are dispersed, Deficiencies tonified. Hot problems are cooled off, Cold problems are warmed up. Dry problems are moistened, Wet problems are drained. This differs from allopathy, which suppresses or excises the symptoms of the problem, from naturopathy, which relies entirely on cleansing, and from homeopathy, which administers an infinitesimally minute quantity of something that has the same nature as the disease process.

Four Natures

The first property of foods is what is called the Four Natures. These are Hot, Warm, Cool, and Cold, referring to the food's effect on the patient's metabolism and physiology. Hot foods create more warmth in the body and cold foods cool down the body. There is a fifth category, neutral or mild, for foods that neither heat up nor cool down the body but maintain a thermodynamic status quo. The *Nei Jing* expresses Chinese Medical heteropathy when it says, "If it is cold, heat it. If it is hot, cool it."[13] Therefore warm and hot foods are used to treat a cold or cool disease. Temperature can be a primary characteristic of a food, as an unchangeable characteristic unaffected by preparation or storage. Or, it can be a secondary characteristic which may be modified by preparation or method of storage.

Taste

The second property of any food is its flavor or taste. There are six flavors. These are salty, sour, bitter, sweet, pungent (acrid or spicy), and neutral. Each taste has its own function. The salty flavor is regarded as having a softening and descending function. Foods and herbs with a salty flavor are often used as lubricants or to disperse hard accumulations. The sour taste is astringent and absorbent. Foods and herbs of sour taste are often used to treat "loose" problems like diarrhea. The bitter flavor is divided into bitter and drying and bitter and purging. The sweet taste is warming and tonifying and is used to supplement Deficiency. The pungent flavor is dispersing and flowing. It can disperse toxins from the body and aid the circulation of Qi and Blood. The neutral flavor has a diuretic action. Sweet, spicy, and neutral can generally be regarded as Yang flavors. Salty, bitter, and sour are Yin flavors. Five of the flavors are particularly related to the Five Zang or Solid Organs: sour has an affinity for the Liver, bitter for the Heart, sweet for the Spleen, pungent for the Lungs, and salty for the Kidneys.

Four Directions

The third energetic category is known as the Four Actions or Directions: ascending, descending, floating, and sinking. A food can make energy go up or down, move to the periphery or to the core. Some herbalists further describe the actions of transformation, giving birth, growth, harvesting, storing, and completion. In general Hot, Warm, and Yang flavored foods tend to move the energy up and out. Cold, Cool, and Yin flavored foods tend to move the energy down and inward. Foods that are light, like leaves and flowers, tend to make energy rise or float. Heavy foods such as seeds, roots, and fruits tend to make energy descend or sink.

Meridian Route

The fourth category is the meridian route. Since the 13th century Chinese herbalists have endeavored to describe which meridian or meridians the energy of a given herb or food predominantly enters. This is a fairly late addition to the energetic theory of foods and herbs and it has largely been deduced through inference. If a certain food helps a certain problem which we know is due to an imbalance in the Liver, then it is logical to assume that the food "goes to the Liver." However, since there are a number of ways to understand the energetic etiology of a given pathology not all herbalists agree on all the meridian pathway ascriptions. Even so, this has been a standard classification of most foods and herbs since the Ming dynasty and continues to be useful.

Yin/Yang Balance

The Yin/Yang balance of a food is the generalized or predominant nature of the food seen from the perspective of dichotomy.[14] It is the fifth category but is not often used in clinical practice.

Five Element

The sixth category is the Five Element ascription of a given food. This also is not frequently used, but is employed more often than Yin and Yang. Some foods are both Yin and Yang, likewise some foods embody a mixture of two elements and, even more rarely, three. As the reader will note, the Yin/Yang and Five Element ascriptions are mostly based on temperature and taste, the two most important energetic characteristics of a food.

Theoretical Function, Symptomatic Effect, Clinical Use

The seventh category is the theoretical function of food. This refers to the therapeutic principles of classical Chinese Medicine. It is an abstraction of the generalized effects of food on the *energetic* physiology. This is amplified and expanded by the next or eighth category, symptomatic effect, which is usually several specific physiologic effects stated in biological parlance. This is in turn followed by the common clinical use of the food stated in pathophysiological terms.

Contraindications

To complete the picture of the medical properties of any food or herb, there is a tenth category, that of the food's contraindications. These are just as important as the indications, since the first rule of therapeutics is *First Do No Harm*. Such contraindications are often overlooked in western presentations of dietary and alternative therapies. If a medicine is powerfully good, but used the wrong way, it is also capable of being powerfully bad.

The Appendix *Categorization of Foods* lists over one hundred foods. Most, if not all, are commonly found in American health food stores or groceries. Some of the more specifically Oriental foods can be found in many Oriental food shops across the nation. Of course, there are many foods which we Americans eat that are not common to Asia and therefore Chinese medical descriptions are not yet available. Determining their energetic nature is one of the tasks at hand for practitioners of Chinese medicine in the United States. It will, however, take several generations to be really sure of such descriptions. Personally I do not accept as more than tentative any descriptions of American foods and herbs by first generation American practitioners with only a few years experience. Nonetheless, if Chinese-style medicine is to take root here in the United States we must learn to use its categories to describe our experience. The Vietnamese, Japanese, and Korean doctors who returned to their countries after studying in China were successful in just this endeavor.

For most of the foods listed in the Appendix, entries for all categories are complete. Most of the temperatures and tastes seem reasonable. I have not included on this list any food for which temperature and taste have not been determined "in the literature," since these are the two ascriptions which make this Chinese system unique. Only a few temperatures or tastes seem contrary to what one would expect. It is necessary to keep in mind that the temperature is the food's net effect on the metabolism. Most foods on the list relate to the Earth element. This is only natural since food itself and the act of eating relate to Earth and the Stomach/Spleen/Middle Burner.

Many foods are listed as tonifying the Qi and Blood. This is an energetic way of saying that the food is nutritive and nourishing. There is also a group of principles that often appears together: Benefitting Qi, Removing Blood Stagnation, Expelling Cold, and Sedating Yin. In general, this means that the food activates both Qi and Blood circulation, relieves stagnation and congestion, and improves function as opposed to building substance. The principle of Regulating Qi means to control the Qi from flowing in a contrary direction such as Up-flushing of Rebellious Stomach Qi in hiccoughs and vomiting. Often the principles listed for a particular food are numerous and may even appear contradictory. In such cases the reader should note the common clinical use of the food to determine the most important principles.

Unfortunately, Dr. Henry Lu, whose *Doctor's Manual of Chinese Medical Diet* is a main source for the *Categorization of Food* Appendix, does not include any bibliography or footnotes for this material. Therefore it is difficult to check its accuracy. It would seem from the way the material is arranged in his work that various sections have been translated from different sources. To me, it appears that he has not edited and presented an amalgamated synthesis but only a collection of information. Such a synthesis is in fact what this present work has attempted to achieve. Dietary therapy is a very important part of health care and both practitioner and patient need easy access to this information.

Therapeutic principles are the logical bridge between diagnosis and treatment and thus between a food's energetic nature and its clinical use. Although the therapeutic principles may help a clinician employ a food in a new therapeutic way, these principles should not be divorced from clinical experience. In principle a food may be good for a certain ailment, but in practice its effect may be negligible.

If a food seems to be appropriate in terms of one or more categories but inappropriate *vis-a-vis* another, the practitioner must rely on his or her discrimination of the most important effects of the food, the most important needs of the patient, the severity of the patient's case, and the impact any logically deduced side effects may have on the patient. The characteristics of a food may be affected, augmented or offset by the amount, preparation or combination with other foods. All these factors should be taken into account when considering any food whose energies are not totally harmonious.

Readers are cautioned not to apply the foods listed on a purely symptomatic basis. Chinese medicine is based on an energetic view of health, a view diametrically opposed to western biology. It is in fact a deeper and more fundamental view of incarnation. Attempts to understand or employ Chinese medical techniques and concepts in terms of western science only serve to destroy the strength and vitality of the Oriental system.

When American patients ask about dietary supplements such as vitamins, minerals, amino acids, or about how much protein they need and where they should get it, they underscore a basic prejudice in favor of the materialistic, scientific world view. From the view of traditional Chinese medicine concepts such as protein and vitamins *are not necessary*. This is not to say that from a scientific point of view proteins and vitamins are not necessary for life. What this means is that if one follows Chinese dietary theory according to its own energetic concepts and principles, one will achieve health without having to consider such materialistic concepts. One will be getting a well-rounded diet even from a western nutritional point of view.

Some readers may ask, why not incorporate western ideas on nutrition into the Oriental system? Why not add the concepts of vitamins and minerals to make the system more complete? Why not have the best of both worlds?

It is my belief and experience that from a pragmatic perspective the materialistic world view is inherently fallacious. This is not to say that it is scientifically inconsistent and unverifiable by its own methodology, but simply that quantitative and materialistic concepts lead only to more mistaken patterns for living and relating to reality. Ultimately, it is our mistaken relationship to reality that is the cause of all disease and suffering; ultimately, this mistake is a conceptual one. Dividing the living fabric of reality into static and quantitative compartments leads us to arrogantly believe that we can juggle the constituents of life as we please. Concepts such as vitamins, proteins, and calories distance us from a humble appreciation that we are the servants of creation and not its masters. The Oriental energetic description of reality fosters this basically healthy attitude and the western materialistic attitude engenders its opposite.

Not only must both the practitioner and patient understand this ultimately spiritual and ethical dilemma, they must eventually as well entrust their lives to one point of view or the other. They must choose a belief system and act on their belief. They must choose a life of grams, calories, amino acids, and inhuman acronyms such as RDA, MSG, and FDA that eventually lead to AIDS, or a life of Yin and Yang, the Four Temperatures, Six Tastes, and a physiology based on a spiritual cosmology that leads to Enlightenment.

Erecting a Dietary Treatment Plan

As has been stated, the basic methodology of Chinese medicine is heteropathy. For those unfamiliar with the process of Chinese medicine, this section may help clarify this methodology, particularly in terms of diet.

When a patient enters the office or clinic of a practitioner of Chinese medicine, that practitioner's first duty is to make an energetic diagnosis. He or she must name or identify in as clear and precise a manner as possible the pattern or combination of patterns of energetic imbalance manifesting in the patient. Although each patient is unique, over two thousand years of Chinese clinical practice has succeeded in delineating a number of syndromes or patterns of disharmony. It is the identification of such a syndrome which comprises a classical Chinese diagnosis.

The practitioner of Chinese medicine arrives at a diagnosis through a combination of methods. Classically there are four major diagnostic modalities: observation, listening/smelling, questioning, and palpation. Observation means to observe the patient's face, demeanor (their Spirit in literal reference), and carriage. Inspection of any wounds, inflammations, eruptions and excreta, and observation of the tongue body and its coating or fur are also included. Listening and smelling, grouped under one heading, means to listen to the quality of the breath, to any coughing, and to some extent the quality or tone of the patient's voice and to smell any excreta or body odor. Questioning includes taking a patient history and asking the patient about the duration, location, intensity, time of onset and aggravating factors which concern their major complaint. In addition, due to the holistic emphasis of Chinese medicine, a clinician will usually seek to discover the patient's general physiology, including elimination, appetite and eating patterns, sleep, energy level, sweating, menstruation if the patient is a woman, and emotional tenor. In most Chinese clinics this takes about fifteen minutes.

Palpation means to take the patient's Chinese-style pulse on the radial arteries at the styloid processes of both wrists. This is a complex procedure and there are a number of different schools or styles of pulse diagnosis. A detailed explanation of Chinese pulse diagnosis is beyond the scope of this work. Some practitioners may also palpate certain acupuncture points on the body and/or certain regions of the abdomen.

Although instruction in Chinese diagnosis is classically presented in terms of these four modalities, in actual practice the diagnosis of an energetic imbalance is usually based on a combination of the pulse, tongue, and signs or symptoms. Most diagnostic texts distinguish a pattern as the pulse being this way, the tongue being that way and the patient presenting these or those symptoms. A different pattern will have at least one of the following: a different pulse, a different tongue and/or a different set of symptoms. Differentiating the pulse, tongue, and signs and symptoms according to commonly agreed upon patterns is called dialectical differential diagnosis.

For example, if a patient has a brown or purplish tongue, a wiry pulse, a sensation of constriction in the throat, irritability and/or depression, and swelling of the breasts, this combination establishes a diagnosis of Constrained Liver Qi. If the symptoms of either nausea, belching, heartburn, or diarrhea are added, this pattern is further differentiated as Liver Invading the Spleen. A patient who presents a red face and eyes, dry mouth, severe headache, dizziness, anger, insomnia, a red tongue with yellow fur, and a rapid, full, wiry pulse is differentiated as Liver Fire Blazing Upward. All three patients suffer from a primary imbalance of the Liver. Yet each patient's pattern is distinct and must be differentiated for purposes of treatment. No single Liver panacea will rectify all three patterns.

Based on such an energetic diagnosis, the next step for the practitioner is to clearly state the appropriate therapeutic principles. If the Liver is Constrained or stuck, then the proper approach is to release it. If the Liver is Invading the Spleen, then the therapeutic principles are to relax the Liver and tonify the Spleen. If the Liver Fire is Blazing Upward, the correct therapeutic principles are to sedate the Liver and lower the Yang. This statement of therapeutic principle is a simple, logical progression. Its importance is in providing both clarity and a unifying theory for erecting the treatment plan. Experienced practitioners may not take the time either externally or internally to expressly state such a therapeutic principle. They may seem to jump from diagnosis directly to treatment. This is only because they have learned to think in energetic terms. The beginning practitioner is advised to always record in principle what the treatment plan should accomplish.

Chinese medicine as it has been developed theoretically and clinically over the past two thousand years posits a finite number of distinct patterns of disharmony. Each pattern of disharmony has its commonly accepted therapeutic principles. For the most part, these are simply and logically deduced. Some therapeutic principles, however, are based not only on logic but also on actual clinical experience of how the body reacts to both certain disharmonies and to certain treatments. There are some differences in opinion among different schools or lineages of Chinese medicine as to how many syndromes there are for each organ. However, these differences are slight. Those interested in the differential diagnosis of the major syndromes of Chinese medicine should refer to either Manfred Porkert's *Essentials of Chinese Diagnostics* or Cheung and Lai's *Principles of Dialectical Differential Diagnosis and Treatment of Traditional Chinese Medicine*. The latter book is particularly clear in stating the progression from diagnosis to therapeutic principle, although its list of patterns is not exhaustive. Such differentiation of syndromes is a large part of the curricula of most Chinese-style acupuncture schools in the United States. Diagnosis based on differentiating patterns and treatment based on subsequent therapeutic principle is considered the orthodox methodology in Oriental medicine both in the United States and in China.

From the therapeutic principle the practitioner must decide exactly what combination of interventions should be applied to implement the principle or principles. Whatever the practitioner does or counsels the patient to do must embody one or more aspects of the therapeutic principle. In terms of erecting a remedial Chinese dietary therapy, each food that is specifically mentioned by the therapist must be mentioned for a purpose and that purpose must be deduced from the therapeutic principles. Either that food's energy will produce or actualize some aspect of the therapeutic principle and should therefore be included in the diet; or, the food's energy is contrary to the purposes of the therapeutic principle and should therefore not be eaten. In some cases, whole groups or classes of food or methods of preparation may be mentioned because of shared energies. In other cases, individual foods may be selected because of their particular idiosyncratic energy. In any case, each food suggested should embody some aspect of the therapeutic principle and each food contraindicated or forbidden should be forbidden because it is logically or experientially contrary to the therapeutic principle chosen.

Returning to our example of the differential diagnosis of Liver imbalances, for Constrained Liver Qi, one wants in principle to release the flow of Qi. Therefore foods that tend to obstruct the flow of Qi or that harm the Liver should be avoided. Foods that promote the free flow of Qi and that benefit the Liver should be eaten. For Liver Fire Blazing Upward, if the principles are to sedate the Liver and lower the Yang, then foods that calm and cool the Liver and lower the Yang should be selected and foods that would raise the Yang, produce internal Fire, or aggravate the Liver should be avoided.

In order to find what specific foods do according to the principles of Chinese medicine the reader should refer to the list of foods and their energetic descriptions in the Appendix. At first, the beginner may find it cumbersome to skim through each food in order to decide whether it should be eaten or avoided. However, here in America, certain patterns of disharmony are more commonly met in clinical practice. A number of these major common patterns have been described in the following chapter. After some time, the practitioner will become familiar with the energetic nature of most common foods and will also have on the tip of their tongue the basic dietary treatment plans for the most commonly encountered patterns. At that point, reference to a list such as may be found appended to this text will only be necessary to answer a specific question about the advisability of a specific, infrequently eaten food. Most Chinese clinicians with whom I have worked and studied, both in China and America, know the salient foods to eat and avoid for the major syndromes. It is almost never necessary to erect a dietary treatment plan which takes into account each and every one of the over one hundred foods listed in the Appendix.

Thus the method of erecting a Chinese dietary therapy is to begin with an energetic diagnosis differentiating the pattern or patterns of disharmony. Then one proceeds to deduce the correct treatment principle(s) which will balance the imbalance. Once this therapeutic principle is chosen, the practitioner should refer to the Appendix and assess each food's energies in light of this principle. If the pattern involves Cold, then cooling foods should be avoided and warming foods should be selected. If the pattern is Yang Excess, foods that promote Yang should be avoided and foods that sedate Yang should be chosen. If the pattern involves Water Stagnation, foods that moisten or produce Fluids are contraindicated and foods that drain, dry, seep, or move water should be selected. In accordance with the

First Law of Therapeutics, be sure to first eliminate foods that will aggravate the condition. After this is accomplished, add foods that will benefit the condition.

A final guideline in erecting a treatment is not to make the patient's diet too extreme. In a Hot problem do not just prescribe everything Cold or Cooling you can think of for the patient. The extremity of the diet should be balanced with the extremity of the patient's condition. This sort of balancing cannot really be learned from a book but must be learned in the clinic and through experience. The beginning practitioner should be warned against overenthusiasm and a tendency to create a very special or exotic diet for the average patient. This type of moderation is difficult so long as the practitioner is trying to prove either to themselves or to others that they or their art are special.

Case Histories

It is my belief that American practitioners of alternative health care modalities pay far *too much* attention to diet. There are literally hundreds of paperbacks touting this diet or that diet: the Scarsdale Diet, the Pritikin Diet, the Gersonn Diet, the Macrobiotic Diet, and so on. There is no doubt that the commercially promulgated TV diet of sugar, white flour, processed, chemicalized, out-of-season and de-natured food is a disaster in terms of long term health. Yet almost every patient who comes to my office, for almost any problem from bunions to Herpes, wants to know what they can add to their diet to make them well. Less often do they ask what they must eliminate from their diet. This obsession is only an extension of the pill-popping common to the Western medical model, and is itself a failure to recognize that our whole contemporary relationship with reality is flawed.

Such preoccupation with food is indicative of the mechanistic concept of the body and life which is the basis of modern materialistic medicine. From this point of view, the body is a machine and we need to know just what fuel to feed the machine to set it to rights again. It is not that simple. Why we eat what we eat has to do with who we think we are and our real beliefs about the nature and purpose of life. Our preoccupation with diet is indicative of our belief in a quick fix, an external manipulation that will protect us from the need of making a radical change in our selves.

Therefore, I have not included in this work overly numerous case histories. Although I do use dietary therapy in my treatment plans, it is always as a support or adjunct to other therapies such as acupuncture and herbs. Unfortunately it is rare for a person to come in seeking preventive advice. I have had only one case where making a dietary change has completely and comprehensively eliminated the problem for which the patient sought treatment. That case is described below since it is a good example of a case where, had the dietary adjustment not been made, acupuncture or herbs would not have been effective. This case also clearly exemplifies the progression from diagnosis, including identification of the precipitating factor, to therapeutic principle, to treatment plan, and shows how this progression is used in the realm of diet.

A woman in her forties came to my office complaining of breakthrough bleeding between her periods. She was in good health with no previous history of menstrual or gynecological problems. Other than being a little overweight she complained of no other problems, nor could I elicit others in my questioning. Her tongue was somewhat red, her pulse was a little rapid, and the color of the menstrual blood was bright red. Her MD offered no explanation or treatment for her bleeding. From the point of view of Chinese medicine her differential diagnosis was breakthrough bleeding due to Hot Blood.

From treating previous cases of Hot Blood mid-cycle bleeding I knew acupuncture was effective in Cooling the Blood and stopping the bleeding. However, I was not satisfied with making a diagnosis before ascertaining what had caused the presence of abnormal Heat in the Blood. Since this woman was in such good health and spirits I felt it was necessary to find the cause of the Hot Blood in order to eliminate it and prevent its recurrence after her treatment with acupuncture. After discussing her diet and lifestyle for some time it became apparent that the precipitating cause was eating chicken *every day* as part of a special Dr. So-and-so's weight loss diet. Chicken and shrimp are both foods that can cause Hot Blood if eaten to excess over a period of time. Having determined that the cause of her Hot Blood was solely dietary, I simply advised her not to eat any chicken for a while.

From that moment on she had no further breakthrough bleeding. Had I not been able to pinpoint the dietary cause of this woman's Hot Blood and counselled her to avoid this aggravating food, acupuncture and herbs would have been only a symptomatic and ineffective treatment. By pinpointing the cause, I was able to "cure" her of her problem, a problem for which allopathic medicine had no solution, in one session without administering needling treatments or expensive herbs.

Cases such as this one have not been common in my practice. Most of my dietary recommendations are not any more specific than to eat tonifying and nourishing foods and to avoid foods cooling to the Middle Burner Fire, for patients with Deficiency, or to avoid foods that aggravate the Liver, for patients whose problems stem from the Liver. Following, however, is a case history which clearly shows how eating an inappropriate food can have a deleterious effect on an otherwise well-conceived treatment plan.

A young woman in her late twenties was receiving treatment for Stagnant Blood in the Lower Burner due to a history of abortions, Damp Heat obstruction (Herpes genitalia), Liver Qi blockage, and dietary insult to the Liver, Spleen, and Kidneys through eating sugar and coffee. Her allopathic diagnosis was cervical dysplasia. She had had her cervix "frozen" once and it had been recommended that she undergo that procedure again or have a biopsy, since her Pap smears were abnormal. She had premenstrual discomfort, menstrual pain, and her blood flow had progressively diminished, becoming darker and more clotted.

She had been receiving three or four acupuncture treatments prior to the onset of her period for two cycles in addition to daily doses of the herbal formula *Kuei Chih Fu Ling Wan*, also known as Two Peony Root Tea. By the start of the second period since beginning treatment her premenstrual discomfort had been reduced. Her blood flow began a healthy red color without clots and without pain, a definite change for the better. She had been given a general dietary guideline to nurture and nourish the Blood and had been asked to avoid all Liver-aggravating foods. She was having trouble, however, giving up sugar and coffee.

The evening of the first day of her period she was tempted to have some ice cream, which she did. Her blood flow diminished, changed to a darker color, became more clotted, and she began experiencing more fixed, stabbing, Stagnant pain. The next day, she came in for an acupuncture treatment for this pain. Needling SP-6, CV-6, and ST-29 began to relieve the pain immediately. However, when she told me about her ice cream eating escapade the night before, I placed moxa on the handles of the abdominal needles to warm the Cold Obstruction caused by the iced food. This warming technique eliminated the pain entirely and improved the vitality of the blood flow. I have seen other cases of intense dysmenorrhea precipitated by the ingestion of popsicles or ice cream when I worked at the Lung Hua Hospital in Shanghai. This is a clear example of how an inappropriate food "spoiled" or diminished the otherwise positive effect of acupuncture and herbal therapy.

The tendency to overemphasize the remedial and preventive role of diet is well evidenced by the Deficiency states most food faddists eventually manifest. We have mentioned Qi and Blood Deficiency as a probable result of excessively detoxifying and purging diets (raw foods, fasting, or juices). We have also mentioned the deleterious effects on Qi and Blood of excessively salty diets such as are followed by many Macrobiotics. The following case exemplifies the problems that are often caused when individuals are too concerned about diet but are without either adequate theoretical knowledge or clinical experience.

The patient was a woman in her mid-thirties. She was a Macrobiotic nutritional counselor. Her complaints were matitudinal insomnia, lumbar pain, occasional sciatica on the left side, an abnormally lengthened period of 8-10 days, breakthrough bleeding at the full moon, occasional night sweats, dizziness, falling hair, nervous agitation, and some fatigue. Her tongue was most definitely pale, fluted, and had a dry white coating. Her pulse was forceless on both wrists and wiry at the Gate (Guan) position of the left wrist. Her stools were often loose and she sometimes had loose bowel movements after each meal. She was very thin and fragile-looking and her skin was darkish and without lustre. Her voice was groaning and her presentation of symptoms was very scattered.

My diagnosis was Qi and Blood Deficiency with damage to the Jing. There was also some Blood Stagnation which manifested as cold feet, sciatica on the left side, a tendency towards leg varicosities, clotty menstrual blood and some dysmenorrhea. It was my opinion that the majority of her symptoms were due to overconsumption of sour foods in the form of umeboshi plums, sauerkraut, and other pickled foods; and salty foods in the form of umeboshi, seaweed, and gomasio. The excessive salt and sour had harmed her Qi and Blood and had caused Stagnation of Blood in her Lower Burner. Her Kidneys had been adversely effected by the salt and were failing to catalyze the formation

32

of Blood. The Middle Burner Fire had been overly cooled by the salt and the Spleen had become weak as was evidenced by the fluted tongue, loose stools, and the failure of the Spleen to restrain the Blood. The Blood being Deficient, the Shen in the Heart had become anxious since it lacked its proper support. Hence the mental agitation and tendency to matitudinal insomnia.

This patient wanted to know all about this and that food and tried to fit everything into a primitive and incomplete Macrobiotic form of Yin/Yang dichotomy. I prescribed a Blood-building and Middle Burner tonifying diet but emphasized that she should not pay undue attention to her diet and that, in fact, it was her misguided attention to diet which had gotten her into this trouble in the first place. She did not have either sufficient theory or experience to play with her diet, much less counsel others. In addition to emphasizing that she should not pay much attention to her diet other than eating good *quality* foods, I also prescribed a patent female Blood and Middle Burner herbal tonic: Women's Precious Pills (also known as Eight Pearls Pills) since I did not feel that diet without herbal medication could turn her situation around fast enough given the rapid approach of winter. I would have also suggested acupuncture/moxibustion treatments except that she lived too far away to receive these on a regular basis. Such treatments would have helped to more speedily redress the ill effects of her dietary faddishness and to calm her mind.

Some readers may wish I had given detailed dietary regimes for each and every one of the major syndromes of classical Chinese medicine. This would satisfy a certain habit of the Western mind which finds comfort in graphs, tables, lists, and logical equations, *i.e.*, for this problem eat this food and avoid that one. There is, no doubt, a type of security or assurance in such a simple, by-rote approach. However, in this book I have sought to present the principles of the *process* of erecting a dietary treatment plan for Chinese energetic patterns of disease. Also, I have provided a list of specific foods with energetic descriptions that may be matched to the therapeutic principles of an energetic diagnosis. With this information, I have tried to provide the tools and the logic for the practitioner to deduce a diet plan of their own.

Some may find this process opaque. They may not understand or comprehend the procedure. Others may, out of laziness, find it too difficult to go through the process step by step. For both these groups I have no apology. By writing this book I have hoped to clarify how patients and practitioners can *think* about diet in a logical, discriminating way, a way that has been tested by time over twenty centuries. Those who find this logic beyond them are precisely those who should not be fiddling with their own or other peoples' diets. Although I have sought clarity in this presentation, I have tried not to over-simplify a subject which, on the remedial level, is best left to professionals who have been trained in theory and in clinical practice.

Most of the problems besetting mankind are because of our reluctance to *think*, are because of our *willful* ignorance. Hopefully, perceptive readers will proceed in their application of the material presented herein like Prince Wen Hui's cook. When they come to difficulties they will carefully assess the "grain" of the situation, not hurry, compose themselves, and then apply a few deft interventions which will "cut to the core" of the matter. Beyond just being a technique, Chinese medicine and therefore Chinese dietary therapy is a way of approaching life. It is a process or Path, a Tao. As Dr. Zhong Shan wrote in 1933, "One should not look down on the Physician as practicing the little Tao ⟨ a worldly or mundane path ⟩...only integrated with no false character, tranquil and serene, can a person discuss the subject of medicine."

Pa Kang, The Eight Principles

The Eight Principles are the dominant diagnostic scheme of Traditional Chinese Medicine today. According to Ted Kaptchuk, these Eight Principles were introduced into Chinese medicine in the Ming Dynasty (1368-1644) as a way of systematizing and teaching diagnosis. Since Eight Principle diagnosis is currently accepted as the standard it is appropriate that we mention it in relation to diet.

The Eight Principles are: External and Internal, Hot and Cold, Excess and Deficiency, and Yin and Yang. In other words, they are four sets of dichotomies. The nature and location of any disease or imbalance may be described either in the superficial region, caused by an invasion of an Exogenic or External pathogen, or it may be described in the Internal or deep regions. An External pathogen such as Cold or Heat may penetrate to the interior, but most Internal diseases are caused by internal etiologies such as faulty diet, lifestyle or sexual activity. Many diseases manifest as an imbalance in the regulation of a patient's subjective experience of warmth. Therefore, diseases which manifest as an increase of heat are classified as Hot and diseases which manifest as decrease of heat are classified as Cold. This can get complicated, since there are both Excess Hot and Cold and Deficiency Hot and Cold, not to mention False Hot and Cold. When the metabolism becomes disordered and the circulation loses its regularity, various energies in the body may become Excess (too much) or Deficient (too little). Excess and Deficiency can be systemic as in Deficient Qi or Deficient Blood or they may be local as in Excess Damp Heat in the Gallbladder. Exogenous pathogens are by definition Excesses in that they have invaded the body where they are not supposed to be. Yin and Yang are the broadest of the four categories and are used to generalize the other three categories which often occur together. Therefore External, Hot, and Excess are generalized as Yang. Internal, Cold, and Deficient are generalized as Yin. There are specific Yin and Yang energies in the body which may also be referred to in an Eight Principle diagnosis. In this case Yin and Yang are used as nouns, for example, Deficient Yin of the Stomach as opposed to Yin disease.

In the clinic the practitioner often meets cases that fall between the clearly delineated syndromes. Most patients present a mixture of symptoms from several syndromes and manifest a combination of some Excess and some Deficiency. The diagnosis often becomes clear only in the process of treatment. The clear-cut textbook cases one studies in school are reassuring when met, but are not often met. However, using the Eight Principles approach, the practitioner should be able to make some basic discriminations in all cases. Based on these discriminations the clinician should be able to *begin* a provisional course of treatment and at least *rule out* aggravating factors. In other words, a practitioner may have difficulty making a precise diagnosis such as Stagnant Fluid, Rebellious Qi due to a congested Liver, Deficiency of Yang due to Middle Burner and Kidney weakness, aggravated by the easy invasion of Wind Cold due to weak Wei Qi, which is a typical allergic rhinitis scenario. But at least the practitioner should be able to determine that the patient has a Deficiency of vitality or that the problem is an infectious (External) problem and can begin making some simple adjustments.

In the realm of dietary therapy, if a disease is diagnosed as a Cold Disease, cold foods should be avoided and warm foods should be eaten. Foods that are energetically cool and cold are: cucumber, banana, tomato, soy products (such as tofu, tempeh, soymilk), citrus fruit, spinach, seaweed, melon, and millet. Foods that are warm and hot are: squash, carrot, peach, mussel, onion, litchi nut, leek, kidney, mutton, garlic, coconut milk, chicken, chestnut, and amasake.

If a disease is External, foods that open the superficial regions and promote diaphoresis or sweating are indicated, as long as the imbalance is in the Tai Yang or Wei Qi stage of invasion and the person's Righteous Qi is strong enough to undergo such a discharge. Food therapy is not very important in treating External diseases, although it is of utmost importance preventively. As Li Dong-Yuan correctly theorized, the vitality or Yuan Qi responsible for the creation of Defensive energy is directly dependent upon the creation of Postnatal Qi by the digestion. Disease which is Internal is usually the result of factors such as dietary imbalance or lifestyle. Diet is quite important in treating most Internal diseases. However, if the preliminary diagnosis is an Internal imbalance, more precise descriptions of the imbalance are necessary before we can add or subtract any food. There are no foods listed under the general category of Internal since the description Internal is not precise enough to imply any particular treatment principle.

Internal diseases can be further described as Excess or Deficient. If the problem is an Excess, the specific Excess must be defined. If it is an Excess of Liver Yang, an Excess of Liver Fire, or an Excess of Liver Wind, foods that lower the Yang in general are indicated. Such foods are: apple, asparagus, barley, celery, day lily flower, cucumber, eggplant, gluten, mango, mushroom, and pear. Foods that raise the Yang should be avoided. These are: amasake, anchovy, bay leaf, black pepper, butter, cherry, coconut milk, leek, litchi, and mung bean. However, when one attempts to reduce or sedate a pernicious energy in the body one must be very sure not to reduce the Righteous Qi as well. Before attempting to reduce any Excess one should first take into account the extent and nature of any concomitant Deficiencies.

If the problems is a Deficiency it is best if the exact nature of the Deficiency can be defined, for example, Deficient Kidney Yang, Deficient Spleen Qi, Deficient Heart Blood, and so forth. However, even if this is not possible to ascertain, one can immediately specify that only foods tonifying to the Qi and Blood in general should be eaten. These include foods that are warm in nature, but not necessarily hot, foods that are nutritive and nourishing and not eliminative or dispersing, and foods with a generally ascending rather than descending nature. Since the Stomach/Spleen/Middle Burner is the source of all Postnatal Qi, foods that strengthen the Middle Burner, regulate and promote digestion, and support the Righteous Qi should be the basis of any diet used to treat *any* Deficiency.

Yin and Yang as two of the Eight Principles are so general the Chinese do not use them in dietary therapy. In the energetic descriptions of the foods included in the back of this book one will notice that each food is categorized as Yin, Yang, or Yin and Yang. However, I have never seen any clinical use of these categories in dietary therapy in China or amongst Chinese practitioners in the United States. Chinese doctors only shake their heads uncomprehendingly when Americans describe how some believe we can create entire diagnoses and diets based only these two principles. However, foods that tonify or reduce Yang and foods that tonify Yin *are* very important in Chinese medical dietary therapy. Foods that tonify Yang are: radish, raspberry, shrimp, yellow squash, sweet rice, turnips, leek, litchi, fennel seed, coriander, coconut milk, and cherry. Foods that tonify Yin are: millet, mulberry, mung bean, cantelope, nori, octopus, duck, oyster, persimmon, pork, salt, sardine, shark meat, tomato, water chestnut, and watermelon. Foods that sedate overactive Yang have already been mentioned. Care should be taken to distinguish this use of Yin and Yang as nouns denoting specific and diagnosible energies in the body and their use as adjectives, such as is a common practice in Macrobiotics.

Foods that tonify the Yang most often tonify either or both the Kidneys and the Middle Burner. Foods that tonify the Yin usually tonify the Kidneys and in general promote the secretion of internal Fluid. As Chu Dan-xi stated, Yang often is Excess but Yin tends to be Deficient. Therefore Yin, or more specifically the root of Yin, the Kidneys, is never sedated. As Chang Ching-yue correctly pointed out, although Yin is the root of Yang, Yang must activate and motivate the production of yin. Therefore, as the most important dietary guidelines in clinical practice it is wise to pay attention to both Kidney Yin and Yang and to always nurture and protect the Middle Burner.

Common Etiologies and Remedial Dietary Regimes

Hong-yen Hsu in *The Way to Good Health with Chinese Herbs* has given some dietary suggestions in terms of western pathologies. By placing the dietary regimes before the explanation of herbal therapy he has implicitly emphasized the fundamental importance of diet in any remedial treatment plan. However, his decision to use western pathological categories is unfortunate. Hypertension, diabetes, diarrhea, arthritis and bronchitis are all common ailments that American clinicians often see. However, to prescribe a diet for hypertension ignores the fact that there are seven or eight different energetic conditions which might cause high blood pressure. The diet must match the specific etiology and conformation, otherwise it will not be helpful at best and at worst it may prove detrimental.

Naburo Muramoto in *Healing Ourselves* has also give remedial dietary regimes for many common ailments. He has chosen to use a combination of western pathologies and the energetic dichotomy of Yin and Yang. Conceptually this is a step in the right direction. Unfortunately the Macrobiotic definition of Yin and Yang is not consistent and differs from the classical Chinese. The Macrobiotic definition is a product of oversimplification in attempting to describe all illness using only this very generalized dichotomy and the viewpoint *and* prejudices of George Ohsawa, the founder of Macrobiotics. Following Muramoto's advice on some diseases such as hypertension, an individual might in fact eat increased amounts of some foods, such as salt, which would be highly deleterious. Although his introduction of an energetic way of thinking about disease was progressive at the time *Healing Ourselves* appeared in American bookstores, the approach, since it is oversimplistic, is also irresponsible.

The dietary regimes that follow are categorized according to classical Chinese medical syndromes. There are many other syndromes in Chinese medicine, but in my experience, the ones that follow are more frequently encountered in daily practice. Each category is accompanied by a set of symptoms and indications which are the distinguishing factors in differentiating the syndromes. Also included are the western names of pathologies which are often the result of such an energetic imbalance. Once again the reader is cautioned not to use the dietary regimes presented based on the western categories alone. These are only given to allow the westerner an entry point into the energetic way of seeing disease which is deeper, more complete, and less iatrogenic than the allopathic way.

These descriptions assume that the practitioner has a good knowledge of differential diagnosis and the energetic syndromes of Chinese medicine. The patient or lay-person is referred to Ted Kaptchuk's *The Web That Has No Weaver* for a fuller understanding of Chinese medical theory, categorization of pathologies, and the relationship of western pathologies to energetic syndromes.

Stomach/Spleen Deficiency

There are several separate syndromes related to Deficiency of the Stomach and/or Spleen which result in various frequently encountered digestive disorders. Three of the most common are Spleen Qi Deficiency, Spleen Yang Deficiency, and Damp Spleen. Spleen Qi and Spleen Yang Deficiencies are both true or simple Deficiencies. Damp Spleen is an Excess due to Deficiency or a mixed Excess-Deficiency syndrome.

Deficient Spleen Qi means that the day-to-day function of the Middle Burner is impaired. It can be the energetic cause of nervous indigestion, chronic diarrhea, gastric or duodenal ulcers, anemia, and even hepatitis. Its symptoms are poor appetite, abdominal distention, slight epigastric pain relieved by pressure, a tendency to loose stools, fatigue, a pale tongue with thin white fur, and a weak pulse. If this situation is not corrected the patient will not be able to extract the pure Qi from food. Not only will the Spleen function be impaired, but over a period of time there will be a drain on the root energy of the Middle Burner, the foundation of post-natal life and source of Acquired Essence. Thus a Deficiency of Yang, not just Qi, will develop. This is a deeper and more serious imbalance. Because the Yang will have been seriously depleted, symptoms of a cold nature will manifest: fear of cold, desire for hot foods and drinks, desire for warmth (particularly applied to the Middle Burner), and cold hands and feet. The loose stools associated with Spleen Qi Deficiency will further devolve to watery stools possibly containing undigested food. The tongue will be moist, pale, and swollen with indentations on its sides. The pulse will be slow and thready. Besides the pathologies listed under Spleen Qi Deficiency, western pathologies such as leukorrhea, edema, gastritis, enteritis, nephritis, and colitis may be caused by Spleen Yang Deficiency.

In Chinese herbal therapy it is both possible and necessary to prescribe herbs that will specifically treat either Qi Deficiency or Yang Deficiency. Herbs effective in treating Qi Deficiency will not be rapidly effective in remedying Yang Deficiency. In dietary therapy such a degree of precision is not required.

In erecting a dietary treatment plan for either Spleen Qi or Spleen Yang Deficiency, the first principle is to avoid foods that will cool the digestive Fire. Next, you should recommend foods that tonify the Middle Burner. The patient should be advised not to eat any chilled, iced, refrigerated, or frozen foods and liquids. All foods should be room temperature or cooked. Raw food such as fruits and salads should not be eaten. Some fruits may be eaten if cooked in pies or compotes, but one should not eat much fruit even if cooked. All foods that are hard to digest or that are cool or cold should be avoided. Foods that are warming should be the basis of the diet. These should be easy to digest and tonifying. Since the Qi is a Yang function, food should be selected from those which assist the Yang. Since the Stomach and Spleen belong to the Earth Element, Earth Element foods should be selected. Tonifying foods of the Earth Element are almost without exception naturally sweet and are often yellow colored.

Patients often ask me why cold foods should be avoided in Deficiency states and I use an analogy of the Stomach as a pot of soup. If cold foods are put into this pot, the body must supply more energy to heat this "stew" to the temperature required for digestion. This often remains merely theoretical for some patients who come back after a few weeks and ask, "Why can't I eat raw or cold foods?" Recently, however, a patient who works for a solar company told me a story that exemplifies concretely the rationale for eating cooked foods.

This patient mentioned that he was installing solar collectors on a large cattle ranch to both pump and heat water for cattle. I asked why the rancher wanted the water for the cattle heated. He explained that the well water was around 30 or 40 degrees Fahrenheit and that the cows' basal temperature is around 100 degrees. This means that when the cows drink the water they must expend body heat, energy, to raise the temperature of the water by 70 degrees. If the water temperature is raised 70 degrees before they drink it, the cows gain weight appreciably quicker. Since they do not have to burn calories to heat the water in their Stomach, these calories can be used for other purposes, in the cows' case to put on weight. Not only do the cows grow faster but

40

they are more resistant to disease since they have more energy with which to defend themselves.

In terms of digestive physiology, the human Middle Burner is essentially the same as the cow's. Therefore, by eating cooked and room temperature food we humans need to expend less energy to raise the temperature of our food in our stomachs to 98.6 degrees. For my patients who suffer from Middle Burner Deficiency syndromes, this difference in calories is significant.

What should a person with Spleen Qi or Spleen Yang Deficiency eat? Cooked squash, carrot, sweet potato, yam, rutabaga, turnip, leek, onion, and pumpkin (lightly stir-fried, steamed, baked, and/or mashed); well-cooked soft rice, sweet rice, and oats; butter; small amounts of chicken, turkey, mutton, beef or anchovy (particularly broths, soups or gravies of these); cooked peach, cherry, and strawberry; dried litchi and fig; cardamon, ginger, cinnamon, nutmeg, black pepper; tapioca and other custards; kudzu root, arrowroot; and moderate amounts of sweeteners such as honey, molasses, barley malt, rice bran syrup, maple syrup, and sugar. What should be avoided? Salad, citrus fruit and juice, too much salt, tofu, undercooked grain, millet, buckwheat, milk, cheese, seaweed, agar, too much liquid with meals and too much sweet. In the case of Spleen Yang Deficiency, more warming spices may be used, such as cayenne and dried ginger instead of fresh ginger. Food should be eaten in moderate amounts and it should be well chewed. Recipes that are particularly useful in treating Spleen Qi and Spleen Yang Deficiency are given in later chapters.

In some cases, due to functional weakness, the Spleen is not able to metabolize Fluid properly and its function is even further compromised by a build-up of Dampness. This is a complicated case of an Excess of a pathogen produced by an underlying Deficiency. Its symptoms are anorexia, inability to discern taste, nausea, watery stools, heavy headedness or headaches, fullness of the chest, and watery skin eruptions and inflammations. The pulse is slippery or sodden and the tongue fur is thick and greasy. Western pathologies caused by Damp Spleen may include chronic dysentery, chronic hepatitis, chronic gastroenteritis, and also migraine and leukorrhea. Often, since water is accumulating rather than being distributed properly, the patient feels thirsty but in severe cases drinking may cause nausea and even vomiting. In such cases, besides Dampness in the Spleen there is Water Stagnation in the Stomach (ascites).

The principle here is to tonify the underlying Deficiency while at the same time getting rid of the Excess Damp. In general the diet should be similar to that for Stomach/Spleen Deficiency. However, care must be taken not to eat foods that produce more Fluid such as excessive consumption of red meat, sugar, salt, rich foods such as shellfish, dairy products, and excessively watery foods. Foods that drain Excess Damp are indicated: barley, corn, aduki bean, pumpkin, alfalfa, anchovy, chestnut, chicken, and chicken gizzard, garlic, Job's Tears (Chinese barley), kidney bean, kohlrabi, mackerel, marjoram, button mushroom, mustard green, radish, scallion, shrimp, turnip, and white fungus. Foods that produce Fluid and therefore need to be avoided include milk and milk products, pork, shark meat, egg, sardine, agar, asparagus, bamboo shoot, black sesame, carambola, cabbage, clam, mussel, crab, octopus, coconut milk, cucumber, duck, goose, seaweed, kelp, kudzu, olive, soybean, tofu, spinach, and pinenut.

Middle Burner Deficiency may be caused by faulty diet but also by emotional imbalance. Often in such cases, the Chinese diagnosis is that the Liver invades or attacks the Stomach and/or Spleen according to the Control Cycle of Five Element Theory. This is also a mixed syndrome. The Liver is Excess and the Stomach/Spleen is Deficient. This may cause digestive problems such as epigastric pain, belching, hiccough, abdominal distention or chronic diarrhea. A wiry pulse and aggravation of the symptoms due to stress or emotion are the most common differentiating symptoms. In this type of digestive disorder one should tonify the Stomach and Spleen as described and at the same time calm and relax the Liver and promote the unobstructed flow of Qi.

See recipes for: Congee, 82; Spicy Chicken Gizzards and Hearts, 90; Clams with Black Bean-Garlic Sauce, 91; Five-Jewel Casserole, 92; Eight Jade Casserole, 93; Chinese Paella, 95; Chinese Peanut Butter and Sesame Seed Cookies, 97; Kidney/Abalone Saute, 100; Mushu Chicken (Chinese Pancakes), 101; Hwang Chi with Chicken Essence Soup, 102; Quick Preserved Vegetable Saute, 103; Nori Egg Drop Soup, 106; Mushroom Abalone Soup, 107; Oxtail Tomato Soup, 108; Chicken and Walnut Saute, 109; Sweet Potato Porridge, 110; Eight Treasure Rice "Pudding," 113; Mushroom Winter Melon Soup, 114; Sweet Potato Pie, 118; Amasake Cheesecake with Cherry Topping, 119; Shepherd's Pie with Beef or Chicken, 120; Ginger Beef or Ginger Seitan "Beef," 122; Baked Mashed Turnips or Daikon Radish, 123; Corn Spoon Bread Pudding, 129; Delightful Date Bars, 131.

Rebellious Qi and Water Toxin

This syndrome is comprised of several imbalances each of which is subclinical. It is only when the several imbalances manifest together that a clinical problem appears. In this sense, this problem is more a scenario than a distinct syndrome. It is related to Stomach/Spleen Deficiency or Middle Burner Fire Deficiency but is more complicated. Due to stress (from the Seven Passions), Kidney Fire becomes weakened. This is exacerbated by eating foods such as sugar, caffeine, chocolate, and alcohol, which exhaust the Kidney Fire. A chronic attenuation of Kidney Fire leads to less than optimal Stomach/Spleen function. Because the Middle Burner does not metabolize food and fluids completely there is a tendency to create Sputum or mucous, a Fluid imbalance or accumulation. Also, due to stress, the Liver Yang has a tendency to rise. Anger, frustration, and "type A" behavior make the Liver energy rise toward the upper part of the body. This causes a generalized tendency for the Lung Qi and the Fluid from the Middle Burner to ascend. This combination of Rebellious Qi and Water Toxin or Sputum may manifest as allergic rhinitis, watery eyes, sinus headache, or hives when the patient is under stress, is eating an aggravating diet, or is invaded by an External pathogenic energy as is the case in seasonal hayfever or agent-specific allergies such as cat hair or dust.

The underlying symptoms in this scenario are often fatigue, reduced sexual performance, cold feet, an aversion to cold in general, low back and/or neck and shoulder tension, frequent contraction of colds and flu, arthralgia, neuralgia, sciatica, and a large appetite but usually without weight gain. Prominent emotions usually include fear, anxiety, worry, and loneliness, all of which deplete Kidney Yang energy; and anger, frustration, impatience, uneasiness, and generalized tension, all of which exacerbate Liver Yang and further harm the Middle Burner.[15]

In such cases the production of mucous is attributable to weak digestion failing to metabolize Fluid. Sneezing and the symptoms manifesting in the head and chest are attributable to the Rebellious Qi. The susceptibility to invasion by pathogens which are not aggravating to the general population is attributable to the weak Kidney Yang, the source of the Wei Qi. Therefore, the principles of treatment should be to tonify the Stomach/Spleen, transform Sputum, lower the Rebellious Qi, and tonify the underlying Kidney Yang.

Since this scenario is usually the outcome of both dietary indulgence and emotional imbalance, dietary treatment alone is seldom sufficient to treat it effectively. However, without dietary therapy it is impossible to treat. A dietary regime similar to that for Stomach/Spleen Deficiency should be adopted as the basis of the treatment, adding specific foods that transform Sputum. Kidney Yang can be indirectly tonified over time through tonification of the Postnatal Fire, although a judicious use of Kidney tonifying foods is also appropriate. These foods are often organ meats. If the Middle Burner is not digesting well, such hard to digest foods will cause more mucous if eaten to excess. They should only be eaten in small quantities. It is relatively more important not to eat foods that drain the Kidney Yang such as sugar, alcohol, coffee, beer, and citrus juices. Also, foods that aggravate the Liver should be avoided. Foods that produce Fluid should be eaten only in moderation in order to reduce the accumulation of Stagnant Water. If cold and cool foods and liquids and Fluid producing foods are eliminated from the diet, there will usually be a rapid resolution of the mucous and water symptoms. However, tonification of the Middle Burner and the Kidney Yang require consistent dietary and emotional modifications over a protracted period of time. These energies cannot be instantaneously replenished and it is in fact the tendency to demand instantaneous gratification which leads to this syndrome in the first place.

Spleen and Kidney Deficiency

As we have seen, there is a relationship between the digestion, the Postnatal Fire, and the Kidneys, the Prenatal Fire. If one becomes weak, the other will eventually become depleted. The preceding syndrome exemplifies this relationship but in a situation where the various Deficiencies are subclinical until all are added together. However, this scenario of mutual Deficiency of the Middle and the Lower Burner may manifest in more debilitating and life-threatening ways. If a person chronically eats and drinks too much, eats too many sweets which exhaust both the Stomach/Spleen and the Kidneys and eats too many spicy, rich, and fatty foods, a type of Thirsting and Wasting, which western pathology labels diabetes mellitus, may result.

Overeating in general means that the Stomach/Spleen must work overtime. Their function is made more difficult and the energy in the food eaten is not assimilated successfully. Large amounts of liquid are required to keep the contents of the guts fluid. This dampens the digestive Fire. Over time the Stomach becomes Hot and the Spleen Cold. The Stomach becomes like a car stuck in passing gear. The body craves more food in order to get the energy it needs but eating this larger amount only weakens the Spleen's ability to assimilate the essence. The extra fluid must be drained by the Kidneys. Due to over-work the Kidneys become depleted and begin dumping water indiscriminately. This leads to polyuria and a drying out of the body which produces a pathological or false heat. More water is consumed but this only exacerbates the problem. The patient may be fatigued, may have an excessive appetite but be losing weight, may be drinking and urinating constantly, yet be always thirsty. Over time the lower back may become sore and the extremities chilled.

What western pathologists call diabetes is usually categorized as one of seven or eight different syndromes depending upon the indivi-dual signs and symptoms. These are Hot and Cold Wasting, Upper, Middle and Lower Wasting, and combinations of these, as well as Yin, Yang, and Yin and Yang Deficiency Thirsting and Wasting. Middle and Lower Wasting is in my experience the most common Thirsting and Wasting syndrome found in clinical practice in the United States. Besides the symptoms listed above, the patient may complain of ver-tigo, spots in front of the eyes, deafness, impotence, abdominal distention, and watery stools. The pulse in such cases is usually fine and deep and the tongue has a white and greasy coat, which are evi-dence of a chronic situation.

The treatment principles are to warm and tone both the Spleen and the Kidneys. The dietary treatment is similar to tonifying the Stomach/Spleen. Small amounts of food eaten at frequent intervals should be taken instead of large meals. Warming and tonifying foods should be eaten and cooling and cold foods should be avoided. The Kidneys can be tonified indirectly through the Stomach/Spleen or can be tonified directly by eating Kidney tonifying foods. Foods that ton-ify Kidney Yin as well as Kidney Yang should be eaten since the Yin is the foundation and root of the Yang. The first treatment goal should be to firm up the stools. Secondly, the polyuria should be brought under control.

See recipes for: Congee, 82; Oyster-Walnut Casserole, 87; Spicy Chicken Gizzards and Hearts, 90; Clams with Black Bean-Garlic Sauce, 91; Five-Jewel Casserole, 92; Eight Jade Casserole 93; Chinese Paella, 95; Kidney/Abalone Saute, 100; Mushu Chicken (Chinese Pancakes), 101; Abalone Chicken Paste Soup, 104; Quick Braised Soybean Sprouts, 104; Assorted Cucumber and Mung Bean Thread Noodles, 105; Nori Egg Drop Soup, 106; Mushroom Abalone Soup, 107; Oxtail Tomato Soup, 108; Chicken and Walnut Saute, 109; Sweet Potato Porridge, 110; Eight Treasure Rice "Pudding," 113; Mushroom Winter Melon Soup, 114; Shepherd's Pie with Beef or Chicken, 120.

Liver Qi

In the preceding three syndromes, we have discussed Deficiency problems. Liver Qi, on the other hand, is an Excess. In Chinese, Gan Qi means a Stagnation of Liver energy. Liver Qi usually manifests as emotional imbalance such as irritability, frustration, anger or depression. In turn, excesses of any of the emotions can "cause" Liver Qi Stagnation. Its physical symptoms are varied: sensations of a lump in the throat or so-called neurotic esophageal stenosis, distention or lumps in the flanks, groin, or breast regions, lumps in the neck (including goiter), and fibrocystitis of the breasts. The tongue is usually purplish, blue-green, or brown and dark. The pulse is usually wiry or chordal.

There are many western pathologies due to Liver Qi Stagnation. They include dysmenorrhea, premenstrual syndrome, fibrocystic disease, clinical depression, and heartburn. Since Liver Qi is so important in regulating the menstruation more women will notice Liver Qi symptoms and seek treatment. If the Liver Qi invades the Spleen there will be digestive problems such as vomiting, nausea, acid eructation, abdominal distention, flatulence and diarrhea. Although the Spleen's functions are affected, the root of the problem is the Liver Qi. Therefore, these digestive problems can be distinguished by the characteristic "Liver" tongue and pulse signs.

The treatment principles are to spread the Qi and to relax the Liver. The cause of this syndrome is emotional. Diet is usually only an exacerbating factor. Therefore diet is not the main mode of treatment. Dietary modifications will keep the problem from being aggravated and will contribute to a cure. Some "Oriental" dietary practitioners believe that dietary imbalance is responsible for all disease and even for major trends in history. This overlooks the fact that in classical Chinese medicine there are a number of pathogenic factors:

- The Six Evils
- The Seven Passions
- Imbalances or indulgences in lifestyle, diet, sexual activity
- Miscellaneous causes such as trauma, poisoning, insect and animal bites
- Epidemic contagions (Heavenly Retribution diseases)

Usually a person who is imbalanced will manifest that imbalance on multiple levels and often will eat a diet that supports the imbalance. Some people think that their intuition leads them to eat appropriate foods spontaneously. This is true only if a person is in relatively good health. We do not *have* imbalances, however; we *are* imbalances. Once the inertia tips in the direction of the imbalance, cravings usually only magnify this trend. This does not mean that the cause is primarily dietary, nor that in the case of predominantly emotional problems such as Liver Qi, the treatment should be primarily dietary. Diet is lower on the scale of therapeutic intervention. The Mind is primary. If a problem arises in the Mind, then dietary therapy is an indirect or roundabout approach. It is a valid therapy, but not the most efficient.

To relax the Liver, the stress should be placed on avoiding foods that aggravate the Liver. These include alcohol, coffee, excessively spicy foods, heavy red meats, sugar and sweets, and chemicals and drugs, including over-the-counter and prescription allopathic drugs, food additives and preservatives such as MSG and BHT. Besides avoiding specific foods that aggravate the Liver, it is also very important that the patient not overeat in general. Overeating may cause Liver problems and will also exacerbate them. This is true regardless of the quality of the food eaten, although "heavy" foods are more harmful than "light" ones. Some foods that relax the Liver directly are beef and chicken liver, black sesame, celery, kelp, mulberry, mussel, nori, and plum.

Since the strategy is also to decongest the stuck Qi which is causing distention, lumps, and pains, foods that activate or benefit the Qi should be eaten. Many of these are spices and they should not be overindulged or they will further harm the Liver. Qi activating foods include amasake, basil, bay leaf, beet, black pepper, cabbage, coconut milk, dill seed, garlic, ginger, kohlrabi, leek, litchi, longan, marjoram,

47

peach, rosemary, safflower, saffron, and scallion. Many people who are Liver Qi Stagnant tend to eat excessive amounts of garlic, cayenne or green chili sauce because this gives them a rush of circulating Qi. But if the food is too spicy, it harms the Liver, making the problem more recalcitrant.

If the Liver Qi has invaded the Stomach and/or the Spleen, foods that strengthen the Middle Burner should be eaten. Since the digestion is the root of post natal life, the diet suggested for Stomach/Spleen should be considered the foundation of the dietary regime. In my experience, Liver Qi invading the Middle Burner is more common in men than women. Men also tend to experience Liver Qi as emotional disorders without marked physical symptoms and therefore do not often seek treatment until it has devolved to a more severe imbalance.

Ascension of Liver Yang

In men, if Liver Qi is not treated, over a period of time it may devolve into Ascension of Liver Yang, an Excess of Liver Yang energy. For this Excess to develop there must be an attendant diminution of the Liver Yin which would ordinarily keep the Yang in check. However, at the beginning this Yin Deficiency is not pronounced so the syndrome is named for its primary aspect, the Rebellious Ascension of Liver Yang. Further aggravation will lead to Stirring of Endogenous Liver Wind. Liver Yang Excess is commonly found in men, particularly middle-aged men. The symptoms of Liver Yang Excess include irritability, headache, vertigo, flushed face, bloodshot eyes, insomnia, palpitation, lumbar soreness, and weaknesss of the lower extremities. The pulse is wiry and rapid. The tongue tends to be red. The irritability, headache, flushed face, bloodshot eyes, wiry quality in the pulse, and the redness of the tongue are all indicative of an Excess of Yang, that is, Heat. The palpitations, insomnia, lumbar soreness, weaknesss of the lower extremities, vertigo, and rapid pulse are all indicative of Yin Deficiency. Besides insomnia and cephalgia, the most common western pathology caused by this energetic syndrome is hypertension or high blood pressure.

Depending upon which symptoms are most prevalent, one must proportionately adjust the two therapeutic principles of sedating the Liver Yang and tonifying the Liver Yin. If, in fact, there are no signs of Yin Deficiency but more serious Yang Excess signs such as vertigo, splitting headaches, and conjunctivitis with a stronger, fuller pulse, this is Liver Fire Blazing Upward. In this case, it is sufficient to eat foods that are cooling and that lower Rebellious Qi. All foods that aggravate the Liver should be avoided. Foods that cool and suppress the Liver Yang are celery, lettuce, watercress, and seaweed. If there is any accompanying digestive abnormality, it is usually constipation. Therefore, cooling foods can and should be eaten without hesitation, also foods with a strong downward energy such as rhubarb. Without exception, patients with Liver Fire Blazing Upward have a robust constitution. If not, Liver Fire will very quickly transform to Liver Yang Ascension with an attendant Yin Deficiency.

Unfortunately, the generation which is now approaching middle-age lacks a robust constitution, in part because of the poor quality diets we had as children, in part because of lifestyle excesses and ultimately because of the accelerating degeneracy of the Kali Yuga. Therefore, Liver Fire Blazing Upward is not commonly seen in most American acupuncture practices. In the more common Liver Yang Excess syndrome, care must be taken to avoid Liver aggravating foods and to balance foods that cool and lower the arrogant Yang with foods that will support and nourish the depleted Yin. This balance should be based on the relative preponderance of symptoms of Yin Deficiency or Yang Excess. Reducing and cooling foods should be eaten as in Liver Fire pathologies but the amounts should be less. More attention should be placed on eating foods that not only nurture the Yin of the Liver, but also the Yin of the Kidneys, the root of Liver Yin. This syndrome requires a longer course of treatment and the development of patience. The diet must remain balanced over a long period of time. Any quick attempts to cool or suppresss the rising Yang without regard to the underlying Deficiency will only produce diarrhea and lead to a Qi Deficiency and eventual Spleen Deficiency. Such a further complication will only make treatment more difficult.

This problem, like Liver Qi, is due primarily to faulty lifestyle and emotional imbalance. Impatience and frustration, or what some progressive western physicians call time disease, is an integral part of this pattern. The patient is all too apt to seek quick solutions and to go to extremes. Also the patient is likely to seek external solutions to his or her problem, such as supplements, dietary fads, or miracle herbs. This type of patient often employs a shotgun therapy. Usually they are also willful, arrogant, and headstrong. The problem is their self: who they are, not what they eat. It will be hard for the clinician to convince the patient that developing a radically different approach to life is what is required for long-lasting and successful treatment. As our degenerating times accelerate this syndrome and its relatives become more and more prevalent. Already as much as one quarter of the American population suffers from it.

See recipes for: Congee, 82; Buddha's Delight Casserole, 88; Spicy Chicken Gizzards and Hearts, 90, Clams with Black Bean-Garlic Sauce, 91; Spinach with Creamed Crab Sauce, 98; Chinese Tomato Soup, 99; Kidney/Abalone Saute, 100; Mushu Chicken (Chinese Pancakes), 101; Hwang Chi with Chicken Essence Soup, 102; Quick Preserved Vegetable Saute, 103; Abalone Chicken Paste Soup, 104; Quick Braised Soybean Sprouts, 104; Assorted Cucumber and Mung Bean Thread Noodles, 105; Nori Egg Drop Soup, 106; Mushroom Abalone Soup, 107; Oxtail Tomato Soup, 108; Eight Treasure Rice "Pudding", 113; Mushroom Winter Melon Soup, 114; Shepherd's Pie with Seitan (Gluten Meat), 122; Ginger Beef or Ginger Seitan "Beef", 122; Baked Mashed Turnips or Daikon Radish, 123; Leek and Onion Pie, 128; Seitan-Veal Marsala, 129.

The following are several dietary prescriptions for Liver Yang Ascension hypertension which I found in an in-flight magazine aboard a recent trip on CAAC, the Chinese flag carrier. These in turn were cited from a work entitled *Longevity* about which no further bibliographic material was given. I am including these for two reasons: one, because I think they should be effective given the natures of the foods; and two, they clearly underscore the hazy demarcation between herbal formulae and dietary prescriptions.

1) One Cup each of grape juice and celery taken with warm water two to three times per day. Twenty days constitute one course of treatment. This concept of a course of treatment is based on contemporary Chinese acupuncture practice. After a course of treatment the patient is allowed to rest for approximately 5-7 days before resuming treatment. This keeps the organism from becoming habituated to the treatment and also, in my opinion, allows the organism the space to sort things out without being pushed too fast. In most Chinese clinics the Doctor will specify the number of treatments per course and may prognose how many courses will be necessary to achieve the desired results.

2) Ten water chestnuts and 25 grams each of kelp and corn silk, drunk as a decoction (boiled).

3) Soak peanuts in vinegar for 5 days. Eat 10 peanuts every morning.

4) Take a handful of sunflower seed kernels every morning and evening with 1/2 cup of celery juice. Take for one month to achieve the desired results.

5) Take one small "wine cup" of turnip juice morning and evening for 10 days.
6) Decoct 250 grams of celery (approximately 1/2 pound) and drink. At the same time eat 10 large Chinese dates.
7) Soak 6 grams of black fungus in water overnight; steam for one hour; sweeten with sugar to taste. Take one time per day in the evening before sleep until the symptoms and blood pressure have improved.

Blood Deficiency

Blood Deficiency is a commonly encountered syndrome in clinical practice. This is because women seek treatment more often than men and Blood Deficiency is at the root of many gynecological difficulties. In surveys of patient visits and herbal prescriptions filled in Taiwan, the overwhelming majority are for gynecological problems.[16] There is a relative balance between Qi and Blood in the human organism. In general men have more Qi than Blood and properly so, while women should have more Blood than Qi. Men most often suffer from Qi problems and women most often suffer from Blood problems. Symptoms of Deficient Blood include vertigo, thinness or emaciation, blurred vision or spots in front of the eyes, numbness or trembling in the extremities, dry skin and/or hair, a pale lustreless face, a pale tongue body, and a thready pulse. Pale lips, pale undersides of the eyelids, or pale nailbeds are also indicative of Blood Deficiency. Western pathologies and symptoms associated within Blood Deficiency are anemia, palpitations, nervousness, anxiety, amenorrhea, dysmenorrhea, lower back pain, night sweats, and headaches including some types of migraine. Symptoms depend on the relative Blood Deficiency in specific organs such as Liver or Heart. Patients may also present with complications of Qi Deficiency and/or Middle Burner weaknesss manifesting as digestive difficulties. Blood Deficiency can cause a number of serious pregnancy complications and it is during pregnancy, labor, and the puerperium that Blood Deficiency must be carefully guarded against and promptly treated.

The three major organs in the formation of Blood are the Spleen, Lung, and Kidney. The Spleen extracts the nutritive essence from food, "moistens" it and sends it to the Lungs. The Lungs combine this Ying Qi with Fluid and with Jing (Essence) from the Kidneys. This becomes the Xue Qi or Blood Energy. Blood Deficiency is usually

51

the result of Spleen or Kidney imbalance, not Lung imbalance. In most cases, it is a weak digestion caused by faulty diet or emotional stress which leads to Blood Deficiency. Therefore the treatment approach is to tonify the digestion and consequently the postnatal Qi in order to tonify the Blood. Specific foods that tonify the Blood should be eaten, such as mochi (pounded, easily digested sweet rice), mugwort, and liver. If low back pain and darkness under the eyes are part of the symptom/sign picture, Kidney nourishing foods such as oyster, chicken liver, and kidney should also be eaten. Foods that cool or sedate the digestion such as raw fruits and vegetables, iced or chilled foods and liquids, and millet should be avoided. Except for the inclusion of specific Blood tonifying foods, the general concept is the same as tonification of the Middle Burner.

See recipes for Stomach/Spleen Deficiency as well as: Kidney/Abalone Saute, 82; Mushu Chicken (Chinese Pancakes), 90; Nori Egg Drop Soup, 91; Mushroom Abalone Soup, 92; Oxtail Tomato Soup, 93; Chicken and Walnut Saute, 95; Sweet Potato Porridge, 97; Eight Treasure Rice "Pudding", 100; Mushroom Winter Melon Soup, 101; Dragon Eye Pudding, 102; Sweet Rice Congee with Shrimp and Walnuts, 103; Shrimp/Chicken/Water Chestnut and Mushroom Rice Pot, 106; Sweet Potato Pie, 118; Amasake Cheesecake with Cherry Topping, 119.

Stagnant Blood

Although Stagnant Blood can refer to a hematoma caused by a contusion or traumatic injury, in most Oriental medical practices in this country it refers to Stagnant Blood in a woman's lower abdomen. We have seen how Stuck Liver Qi can cause menstrual irregularities, dysmenorrhea, and premenstrual syndrome. The Qi moves the Blood. If Liver Qi congestion is left untreated and the circulation of Qi and Blood in the lower abdomen is generally weakened by abortions, IUDs, or chronic amenorrhea, or by abdominal surgery or suppression of venereal disease by antibiotics (which causes chronic Damp Heat), the Blood may eventually Stagnate. This is a more serious progression, but one that is all too common in the United States today.

There are two types of Stagnant Blood: Insubstantial and Substantial. Insubstantial Stagnant Blood refers to a stagnation of the Blood energy without a palpable mass or lump. It manifests as a number of symptoms such as: dysmenorrhea, amenorrhea, chronic vaginitis, PID, emotional imbalance, dry skin, chapped lips, dark spots on the skin, yellowish complexion, thirst, a tendency to cold feet, constipation, and even chillblains. The menstrual blood is dark and clotty. If this is left uncorrected it will eventually become

Substantial Stagnant Blood. In this case, one can actually palpate a lump or neoplasm in the lower abdomen, most often in the lower left quadrant or on the centerline superior to the pubic bone. Additional Western pathologies which are the result of Stagnant Blood in the Lower Burner include uterine myomas, ovarian cysts, and cervical cancer. In addition to causing many distressing and painful symptoms and potentially leading to life-threatening problems, Stagnant Blood in the Lower Burner can cause a number of complications in pregnancy and in the puerperium. For further information regarding Stagnant Blood as it effects on reproduction see *Path of Pregnancy*.

The treatment principles for Stagnant Blood are to activate the Blood, remove coagulation, and improve circulation in the Lower Burner. Because the Liver meridian plays such an important part in the circulation of the Lower Burner, particularly in women, and because the Qi moves the Blood and the movement of the Qi is regulated by the Liver, it is advisable to avoid Liver aggravating foods. Foods that tend to cause Qi Congestion should be avoided. Foods that improve the circulation of Blood and remove coagulation include eggplant, amasake, saffron, safflower, basil, brown sugar, and chestnut. In order for the Blood to circulate freely it must also be of high quality and in sufficient supply. Blood is manufactured largely as the result of the functioning of the Middle Burner. Therefore foods that depress the Stomach/Spleen function should be avoided and foods that tonify or support the Stomach/Spleen should be eaten.

Unfortunately, the more serious a problem becomes the more specific and technical the treatment must be. Therefore, for treating Substantial Stagnant Blood dietary modification alone is seldom sufficient. Even acupuncture and herbs sometime fail to resolve the problem satisfactorily. However, diet is important as an adjunctive therapy to acupuncture and herbs. In the treatment of Insubstantial Stagnant Blood diet plays a more important role and can achieve more significant results. This is particularly true over a long period of time.

See the recipes for: Congee, 82; Mutton (Lamb) Soup with Tang-kuei, 111; Sesame Dumplings, 112; Eight Treasure Rice "Pudding", 113; Mushroom Winter Melon Soup, 114; Dragon Eye Pudding, 115; Sweet Rice Congee with Shrimp and Walnuts, 115; Shrimp/Chicken/Water Chestnuts and Mushroom Rice Pot, 116; Leek and Onion Pie, 128; Seitan-Veal Marsala, 129.

Fluid Dryness

We have dealt with syndromes typifying imbalance in two of the three humors of Chinese medicine but we have not dealt with Fluid as a separate energetic entity. We saw how Fluid Excess or Water Toxin can be a contributing factor in rhinorrhea and Fluid Excess due to Spleen and/or Kidney Yang Deficiency may cause either local or systemic edema. There is also one Fluid Deficiency syndrome which is commonly seen in clinical practice. This is Fluid Dryness leading to constipation.

Most Americans think only in terms of bulk or fiber when trying to self-medicate for constipation. Although lack of fiber may be one contributing factor in the etiology of constipation, Chinese medicine suggests several others. The most commonly seen are Liver Qi Stagnation, Spleen Deficiency, and Fluid Dryness. We have discussed Liver Qi and Spleen Deficiency. By relaxing the Liver, the Liver's function of promoting patency of Qi flow will release stagnancy in the peristalsis. If the Spleen is weak it may not have the energy to create peristalsis for the transportation of food and liquids. By strengthening the Spleen this torpidity can be tonified.

Fluid Dryness is another cause of constipation. If it is not correctly identified and treated, treatments designed only to promote peristalsis will not be effective. Fluid Dryness is a Deficiency syndrome. It is often part of a larger or more systemic Blood or Yin Deficiency condition in which constipation is only one symptom. However, in some patients it may be the major complaint. It is usually seen in slender women. It is sometimes simply referred to as Deficiency constipation. Its symptoms include vertigo, dry throat, skinniness, white lips, a weak feeling after bowel movements, spontaneous sweating, and even shortness of breath. The pulse may be fine, retarded, or hollow and weak and the tongue may be peeled or fat and tender and light red in color. The specific symptoms depend on whether the Fluid Dryness is part of a larger syndrome such as Blood Deficiency or Yin Deficiency. Depending upon the specific symptoms, the treatment principles include benefitting the Qi, nourishing the Blood, and, most important in relation to the constipation, lubricating the intestines.

We have already discussed dietary tonification of Qi or postnatal energy and tonification of Blood. Using these approaches as the basis for treating Deficiency constipation, foods that lubricate and gloss the intestines should be added to the diet. These foods include apple, pear, honey, clam, cheese, milk, peach, peanut oil, pine nut, sesame oil, and walnut. In addition, foods that tonify the Kidney Yin, the root of Yin in the body, should also be added, for example, pork. The Kidneys rule the Lower Burner. If Kidney Yin has become depleted due to Blood Deficiency, remembering that the Blood is manufactured in part from the Jing of the Marrow, a Yin aspect of the Kidney, the Kidneys will draw out too much liquid from the stools in the intestines, leaving them too dry to pass or to stimulate expulsion.

Most American herbs used as laxatives, such as *Cascara sagrada*, relieve constipation by irritating the Large Intestine so that it is prodded into expelling its contents. In the Chinese medical point of view this approach is only valid for Liver Qi Stagnation constipation in which the peristalsis has become stuck. However, even in that case, if the herb or food only irritates the intestines, without removing the congestion of Qi in the Liver, it will not treat the root of the problem and will eventually harm the intestines. Such an approach will not significantly improve either Spleen Deficiency constipation or Fluid Dryness constipation. In both cases the underlying Deficiencies must be tonified before the cause is remedied. Colonics and enemas lubricate the intestines by mechanical means and this is effective in Fluid Dryness constipation on a symptomatic level. However, these treatments do nothing to replenish the system's depleted vital energies and essences. It is little wonder then that their use can lead to habitual dependence.

See recipes for: Congee, 82; Mutton (Lamb) Soup with Tang-kuei, 111; Sesame Dumplings, 112; Banana-Coconut "Cream" Pie, 133.

Li Dong-Yuan's Theory of Spleen and Stomach

In the two thousand year recorded history of classical Chinese medicine there have been a number of schools or movements, arising over the centuries with the development and expansion of medical theory and experience. In their own era, they were sectarian and even perhaps schismatic. Those however which withstood the test of time were incorporated into the main body of classical Chinese medicine. Such schools include Chang Chung-Ching's Six Layers approach to the progression in External Cold disease, the school of Warm and Hot, the school of Cool and Cold, the school of Tonification of Prenatal Qi, the school of Tonification of Postnatal Qi, and the Four Level approach to the progression of External Hot disease. To readers familiar with these main movements in Chinese medicine it will be apparent that most of the dietary recommendations given in this section are based on the tonification of Post Natal Qi through the Earth Element as classically elucidated by Li Dong-Yuan in the Sung dynasty. This is only natural since most foods belong to the Earth Element and the digestive organs and processes are all ascribed to Earth. It is my experience that dietary therapy, both preventive and remedial, should be based primarily on this perspective of Chinese medicine. This does not mean that particular foods in specific cases should not be administered from the point of view of one of the other schools or theories, for example tonification of Prenatal Qi or Cooling Fire, but that as a general motif, tonification of Postnatal Qi is the most readily applicable and appropriate function of dietary therapy.

Wei Qi Deficiency

Wei Qi is the Defensive energy of the body. It protects the individual from external invasion by any of the six cosmopathogenic or exogenic energies: Hot, Cold, Dryness, Dampness, Wind, and Fire. It flows through the superficial layers of the body in a diurnal cycle. It is strongest on the outside at noon. In the evening it retreats to the core leaving the outside more vulnerable to attack. The Wei Qi is brought to the surface by the Eight Ancestral Meridians and has a close connection with the Yuan Qi which is also circulated by these Extraordinary Meridians. Wei Qi is a Yang energy. It is volatile, aggressive and basically warm in nature. It is responsible for opening and closing the pores and therefore is closely associated with perspiration. Wei Qi is circulated under the controlling influence of the Lungs but its production is based on digestion and the relationship of digestion with the Kidneys and the intestines.

The Stomach separates the pure and impure from ingested food. The pure essence, the flavor, is moistened and transformed by the Spleen to become the foundation of the Postnatal Qi, the Ying or Nutritive Qi. The impure is sent down to the intestines. In the intestines the impure is again separated into pure and impure. The pure of the impure is reabsorbed by the Internal Duct of the Triple Heater. It is sent to the Kidneys, which rule the Lower Burner, and is transformed into Wei Qi. From there it is sent to the Liver, Minister of Defense of the body, to be circulated to the periphery. Therefore, the creation of Wei Qi depends on a strong functioning Stomach and Spleen, correctly functioning intestines, and correctly functioning Kidneys.

If the Wei Qi is Deficient it allows for easy and frequent penetration by external pathogens. Because the Lungs are the "tender" organ according to Chinese medicine, they are most easily invaded or infected by such pathogens. This results in the common cold, tonsillitis, upper respiratory problems, allergies, and influenza. Wei Qi is characterized by only one aberrant syndrome: Deficient Wei Qi. However, no particular illness is attributed to or described as a Wei Qi Deficiency. Wei Qi Deficiency is usually a subclinical situation. The presence of Wei Qi Deficiency is determined by the frequency with which one catches cold. If one easily or frequently catches colds or flu, a Wei Qi Deficiency may be inferred. Since the Wei Qi is part of the Yang Qi, the patient may also exhibit cold extremities, fear of cold, easy chilling, pallor, fatigue, and/or lack of sexual desire. Diagnosing a Wei Qi Deficiency is largely a preventive matter, since once an invasion has taken place the external pathogen must become the primary focus of treatment.

The treatment principle for tonifying the Wei Qi is to tonify the Yang in general by tonifying both the Middle Burner and the Kidney Yang. This means, in terms of diet, avoiding cold or cooling foods and avoiding eliminative and diaphoretic foods. It is important that the Middle Fire be well supported to create more Righteous heat in the body. It is also important not to allow or promote sweating. Qi and Liquid form an interdependent Yin/Yang pair. If a Wei Qi Deficient person is encouraged to sweat, due to the further loss of Qi attending the discharge of Liquid, the condition will become worse. Therefore, fresh ginger would be relatively bad for such a person in large quantities but dry ginger would be good. Huang Qi or Astragalus is the main herbal remedy for nourishing the Wei Qi. Astragalus is often used in tonifying meat broths, sometimes in combination with ginger and either Ginseng or its cheaper and safer cousin, Tang-shen. An example of such a soup is is found on page 102. Leek soup is also good for tonifying the Yang and particularly the Wei Qi. Another home remedy for tonifying the Wei Qi is a broth made out of white onions and unrefined brown sugar, which is warm in nature as opposed to the cool nature of white, refined sugar. However, these remedies should not be used after one has caught a cold. Tonification of the Wei Qi at such a point, closing tight the surface, would lock the pathogen inside the body like a thief in a house, and would lead to a definitely more dangerous situation.

Once again we see the importance of cooked, nutritious, warming, easily-digested foods such as vegetables, well-cooked grains, and small amounts of animal protein. Excessively salty food should be avoided since it leads the energy down and in while the Wei Qi basically flows up and out to the surface. Excessively sweet food is cooling and dispersing of the Middle Burners and the Kidneys, and should also be avoided.

AIDS (Acquired Immune Deficiency Syndrome) begins as a Wei Qi Deficiency. Lifestyle, improper sex, and the use of drugs all contribute to a potential Wei Qi Deficiency. I am not saying that AIDS is solely due to faulty diet. Diet can play a part both in the cause and the treatment of this disease, particularly in the initial phases. By understanding the role, generation and effect of food on the Wei Qi even the average person not at risk for AIDS can prevent a string of debilitating and annoying colds and flu.

Lung Syndromes

The Lungs are called the tender organ in Chinese medicine because they are the internal organ most susceptible to external invasion. Some schools of acupuncture, such as the Worsley school of England, do not treat such External infectious diseases as the common cold. However, Chinese medicine does treat the full range of upper respiratory diseases quite successfully. Diet can and should play a supporting role in the treatment of the various energetic syndromes which usually describe upper respiratory illnesses.

Western medicine divides upper respiratory illnesses into categories: common cold, influenza, bronchitis, asthma, pneumonia, and emphysema. In my experience the most commonly encountered Chinese medical syndromes are Wind Cold invasion of the Lungs, Lung Phlegm, Hot Lungs, Lung Yin Deficiency, and Lung Qi Deficiency. Often, as an upper respiratory disease worsens or runs its course, one can track a progression from the first through the last of these syndromes.

Wind Cold invasion of the Lungs corresponds to the typical common cold or flu caught during the Fall, Winter, and early Spring. In Summer one must take care to distinguish Wind Cold from Wind Heat. Due to wearing less clothing, sleeping without blankets, leaving the windows open, and more frequently sweating without covering or protection, Wind Cold can be caught in the Summer as well. Typically a Wind Cold invasion starts with a sore throat, runny nose, sneezing, headache, aches, pains, and chills. There is often a fever without sweating, but the patient notices being cold more than the heat of the fever. In this syndrome the invading Evil Qi is still quite superficial. It has obstructed the flow and function of the Wei Qi as is indicated by the lack of sweat, headache, muscle aches, and pains. It has begun to disrupt the normal function of the Lungs in the Lungs' periphery: runny nose, sneezing, and sore throat. The treatment principles are to support the body's Righteous Qi, open the pores, and move the Evil Qi out of the body by inducing perspiration. This principle is only appropriate if there is no perspiration and the symptoms are only twelve to twenty-four hours old. At this point there is usually no coughing since the invasion has not moved downward into the Lungs.

Because the invading Evil Qi is Cold, warming foods should be eaten and cold foods should be avoided. For an Evil Qi to break through the protective barrier of the Wei Qi, the body's Righteous Qi must have been Deficient. Therefore warming, easily digested, nourishing foods should be eaten to strengthen the Righteous Qi. However, tonics such as Ginseng or even foods such as scallions and onions are contraindicated during the initial phase of an External invasion. The sudden tonification of the Wei Qi may seal the pores, tightly trapping the Evil Qi inside the body. Eggs are also contraindicated in all Wind diseases. Soups, porridges, meat broths, and other nutritious and easily digested warming foods are most appropriate, just the foods our mothers instinctively fed us when we were sick as children. Specifically, a strong broth made of fresh ginger and brown sugar may be drunk to promote sweating. One should receive a massage (without oil) and go to bed under alot of covers to promote perspiration.

As we all know, although we immediately minister to a cold at its first signs, it often progresses even if we correctly applied sweating. Although this therapy can weaken the pathogen and cut the course of the illness in half, it does not always stop the problem from proceeding further. Often some of the Evil Qi will invade the Lungs. As this happens the symptoms undergo a change reflecting the transformation of the pathology. Depending on the person's constitution and condition either one of two syndromes is likely to develop, or both may develop sequentially.

The first syndrome is Lung Phlegm. This is characterized by the appearance of excessive mucous with wet, productive coughing. Here the treatment principles are to resolve the Phlegm, regulate the Lungs and relieve the cough. Foods that are Damp in nature and generate Liquids, for example, milk and dairy products, should be avoided. Other such foods are soy products, coconut, sugar, sweet rice, persimmon, pork, almond, honey, and peanut. Foods that resolve Phlegm, such as marjoram, mushroom, mustard green, strawberry, string bean, papaya, potato, pumpkin, radish, agar, garlic, fresh ginger, Job's tears, kohlrabi, and tuna should be eaten.

Lung Phlegm can be further divided into Cold and Hot Phlegm. Usually the pathogen begins as Cold Phlegm and transforms to Hot Phlegm. This derives from Liu Wan-Su's theory which became the School of Cold and Cool. Liu Wan-Su observed that when people get sick, particularly when attacked by Exogenous factors, they tend to produce pathological Heat due to similar transformation of energy, since the life of the body is essentially Fire. Cold Phlegm is viscid and white. Hot Phlegm is yellow and green. In treating Cold Phlegm warm herbs and foods are used. In treating Hot Phlegm one must be more careful. One should not eat an overabundance of cold and cooling foods but take herbs and foods that specifically cool the Lungs, for example, Gypsum. Phlegm is resolved by the Stomach and Spleen. Therefore, a Stomach/Spleen/Middle Burner diet should be the foundation of the dietary treatment.

The tendency of people who are already Damp is to produce Phlegm when their Lungs are invaded. In some cases a person will not produce much Phlegm but will complain of fever and have a harsh, dry, unproductive cough, an extremely painful sore throat, and may cough up some blood or scant, dry, yellow Phlegm flecked with blood. This is more typical of Fire in the Lungs or Hot Lungs where the Cold has transformed into Heat without producing an Excess of Phlegm. In this case, the principles are to cool the Lungs, nourish and regulate the Lungs and to relieve the cough. One food that is specific for this condition is white fungus. Agar, celery, asparagus, apple, pear, carrot, duck, Job's tears, mango, shark meat, mushroom, nori, octopus, papaya, peach, persimmon, pumpkin, radish, and rice congee with carrot or aduki bean are all recommended in the treatment of Hot

Lung. Garlic, fresh ginger, pork, mustard green, sweet rice, sugar, and walnut are all contraindicated.

Since Heat tends to harm Fluid by drying it out, if a Hot Lung Phlegm syndrome lasts long enough it will transform into a Hot Lung syndrome. Eventually the Heat will harm and exhaust the Lung Yin associated with the Fluid. If the Lung Yin has been damaged this in turn can cause Lung Qi Deficiency. Lung Yin Deficiency symptoms are a weak, chronic dry cough, a low-grade sore throat, a tendency towards tidal or afternoon fever or flushing, night sweats, a worsening of the symptoms as evening approaches, and thirst. This is a more subtle syndrome. It is not severe enough to demand immediate relief, or so many patients mistakenly believe. Rather, it is a long and drawn-out condition, and does not seem to go away. Most people experience this syndrome as an inability to recuperate and return to their previous state of health. The treatment principles are to nourish and water the Lung Yin and to relieve the cough. Moistening foods such as dairy products are suggested. Pears and apple sauce are also excellent. Other foods that help treat Deficient Lung Yin are seaweed in small quantity, shark meat, watermelon, mutton, tangerine, pine nut, chicken broth, clam, barley malt, walnut, yam, peanut, and chicken egg. The background diet should be a good Middle Burner diet to which antitussives, moisturizers, and Lung tonics should be added. I am **not** suggesting a diet of pears. The Lungs are the child of the Stomach/Spleen and a Stomach/Spleen oriented diet is very important in the treatment of Lung disorders if the mother is to nourish the child.

Finally, depending upon the patient's constitution, Lung Heat may lead to Lung Qi Deficiency, or Lung Yin Deficiency may lead to Lung Qi Deficiency. Lung Qi Deficiency is also experienced as a lingering, prolonged recuperative tardiness. One feels like they should be better but does not seem to be getting any better. For most patients, this is frustrating and upsetting. Lung Qi Deficiency is characterized by a weak, chronic cough which gets worse with any physical exertion, fatigue and lack of energy, a tendency to sweat on slight exertion, and shortness of breath. The principles are to tonify the Qi, nourish and regulate the Lungs, and again relieve the cough.

As in so many previous cases, a Middle Burner diet which supports the production of Postnatal Qi is the foundation of the dietary treatment. Qi tonics such as Codonopsis and Astragalus can be cooked in various soups. Specific foods that are recommended in the treatment of Lung Qi Deficiency are carrot, duck, celery, garlic, fresh ginger, grape, honey (if no sputum), Job's tears, kohlrabi, tuna, barley malt, mango, mushroom, marjoram, mustard green, olive, papaya, peach, peanut, pork, pumpkin, rice, and yam. Any foods that harm the Lungs should be avoided. Any foods that deplete the Righteous Qi should also be avoided. This would exclude the use of any foods that tend to produce diarrhea such as rhubarb.

Colds, flu, and bronchitis are common complaints. During the Fall, Winter, and Spring they are a noticeable part of a practitioner's case load. Although the antibiotics of western medicine are highly touted and ubiquitously prescribed, Chinese medicine is more effective for treating these problems, since it not only attacks the Evil Qi but also places primary emphasis on maintaining the Righteous Qi. Diet, the support of the Middle Burner, is the most important method of protecting and nourishing the Righteous Qi.

See recipes for: Congee, 82; Oyster-Walnut Casserole, 87; Chinese Paella, 95; Chinese Peanut Butter and Sesame Seed Cookies, 97; Spinach with Creamed Crab Sauce, 98; Chinese Tomato Soup, 99; Nori Egg Drop Soup, 106; Mushroom Abalone Soup, 107; Oxtail Tomato Soup, 108; Chicken and Walnut Saute, 109; Sweet Potato Porridge, 110; Eight Treasure Rice "Pudding", 113; Mushroom Winter Melon Soup, 114; Sweet Potato Pie, 118; Amasake Cheesecake with Cherry Topping, 119.

Kidney Yin Deficiency

One of the four great Internal theoreticians of the Jin-Yuan dynasties, Chu Dan-Xi, stated that Yang is by nature often Excess and Yin is by nature often Deficient. Chu Dan-Xi became the founder the School of Watering Yin. He felt that it was very important both remedially and preventively to nourish Kidney Yin. It was Chu Dan-Xi's teacher, Li Dong-Yuan, who developed the concept of Deficient Heat. When the Yin becomes Deficient the Yang which is kept in check by the Yin begins to glow. This glow can turn into a blaze if left unchecked and may cause an upward Internal Draft which further fans the flames. This blaze then even further evaporates and exhausts the Yin. Such a scenario is all too common in our society and in our times.

We have examined the Liver Yang/Kidney Yin connection in our discussion of Ascension of Liver Yang. However, the exhaustion of Yin and the glowing of Yang can produce two other common syndromes, one affecting the sex and the other affecting the Spirit. The

Kidneys and the Heart are connected by the Chong Mo or the Thrusting channel. The Kidney Water keeps the Heart Fire in check. However, the Kidney Fire is the source of the Heart Fire. The Kidney is also the storehouse of the Jing or Essence which includes sexual essence. The Heart is the home of the Shen or Spirit or mind. The Kidneys are the root of Yin and the Heart is the purest, highest expression of Yang: consciousness. Their mutual interdependence *is* the play of life and their separation, well described by Chang Chung-ching as the Jue Yin level of disease, is the process of death.

If the Kidney Yin becomes weak and is the prominent or more severe component of a mutual loss of balance between Yin and Yang, Kidney and Heart, it will manifest as premature ejaculation, spermatorrhea, nocturia, and low back weaknesss. If the Deficient Fire in the Heart is more pronounced, this will manifest as palpitations, irritability, mental instability, insomnia, hyperactivity, and loss of memory. In most cases there will be elements of both of these groups of symptoms. The general principles of treatment are to tonify the Kidneys, water the Yin, reduce the Deficient Fire, and calm the Spirit. Depending on the proportion of Yin Deficiency to Yang Excess, varying weight should be given to these four principles when erecting a treatment plan.

Diet is rarely the sole cause of this scenario, but is almost always a contributing factor. Li Dong-Yuan correctly understood that Deficiency in general often leads to Deficient Heat. (Care should be taken to distinguish Deficient Heat or Deficient Fire from Deficiency *of* Heat or Fire.) As the body runs down it gets overheated as well. Li Dong-Yuan attributed Deficiency largely to a lack of harmonious functioning of the Middle Burner. In particular, excess sweets, alcohol, stimulating foods, and cold foods impair Middle Burner function. In addition, sweets, alcohol, and stimulating foods also weaken Kidney Yin and exacerbate Deficient Fire. This is not a true flourishing of Kidney Yang but a tenuous, strung-out, easily burnt-out glowing of Kidney Yang. Such dietary excesses in turn aggravate lifestyle excess: too much stress, too much thinking, too much sensory input and excess such as sex under the influence of Kidney-weakening agents like alcohol and drugs, masturbation, and promiscuity.

Therefore, in the treatment of Kidney Yin Deficiency with flaring of Deficient Fire, the first dietary modifications should support and nurture the Middle Burner. Secondly, when Kidney symptoms such as premature ejaculation, low back pain, and nocturia are prevalent,

Kidney tonic foods appropriate to the symptoms should be eaten, such as chestnut and lotus seed for premature ejaculation and spermatorrhea. When the Mind housed in the Heart is more prominently disturbed, foods that lower the Yang and calm the Mind should be emphasized. Barley, beef broth, celery, asparagus, apple, banana, and lettuce all lower hyperactive Yang. Longan, oyster, rice, rosemary, wheat, wheat germ, and mushroom all have a calmative effect on the Mind.

If this syndrome or scenario is not remedied it will worsen. Due to the interrelationship of the Yin and the Qi, Qi Deficiency will eventually develop. If this condition is allowed to deteriorate, it will become Yang Deficiency. At this point the patient will be suffering from both Yin and Yang Deficiency. In a sense, the Yang becomes so attenuated from its source, the Yin, that it it too collapses. In such a case the Yang must be supported, again, through the Middle Burner with some attention directed to the Kidneys. However, at this juncture diet alone is not an adequate therapy. Herbs and acupuncture are recommended, supported by a tonifying diet. When the Yang becomes weak, premature ejaculation is transformed into impotence. Due to the relationship between Kidney and Spleen Yang, cocks-crow or matitudinal diarrhea may also develop.

See recipes for: Spicy Chicken Gizzards and Hearts, 90; Clams with Black Bean-Garlic Sauce, 91; Five-Jewel Casserole, 92; Eight Jade Casserole, 93; Kidney/Abalone Saute, 100; Mushu Chicken (Chinese Pancakes), 101; Chicken and Walnut Saute, 109; Sweet Potato Porridge, 110; Mutton (Lamb) Soup with Tang-kuei, 111; Sesame Dumplings, 112; Eight Treasure Rice "Pudding", 113; Mushroom Winter Melon Soup, 114; Sweet Potato Pie, 118; Amasake Cheesecake with Cherry Topping, 119; Shepherd's Pie with Beef or Chicken, 120; Tuna Stuffed Peppers, 126; Lamb Kidneys Andalusian, 127.

Damp Bi Syndrome

Bi in Chinese means obstruction. A Bi syndrome refers to an obstruction in the flow of Qi and Blood in the channels and collaterals. Chinese medicine divides diseases into organ problems and channel or meridian problems. However, for a meridian to be invaded or obstructed by an Evil Qi the body must be Deficient or malfunctioning in some way. From a western point of view, Bi syndromes are musculo-skeletal problems usually involving the joints: rheumatism, arthritis, neuralgia, bursitis, and tennis elbow are usually diagnosed as Bi syndromes. Wind, Cold, Damp, and Heat are the four Evil Qi which are classically described as potential meridian obstructors. In my practice I find that Dampness is the most common obstructing energy to cause joint pain in middle-aged women, particularly those who have a tendency to be overweight. Such patients have made up a significant proportion of my practice.

According to the Eight Principles, Damp Bi syndrome is an Excess problem. However, this Excess Damp is most often precipitated due to an Internal Deficiency. It also typically accompanies a Damp Spleen. The patient is overweight with poor muscle tone. Their skin and flesh feels loose and flabby. They often have cellulite and may sweat profusely and have a tendency to loose stools. The affected joints tend to be puffy and swollen and the discomfort worsens with damp weather or in a damp environment. This Dampness has not invaded the meridians from outside but rather has "dripped down" from the torso. Dampness is heavy and tends to sink. Therefore, this class of patients most often complains of soreness in the knees and the pain is described as heavy, diffuse, and sore rather than sharp, cutting, or piercing. The fact that external Dampness aggravates this condition is due to the similar transformation of energy, that is, like aggravates like.

Besides Damp Spleen dietary recommendations, foods that open the meridians and clear obstruction should also be eaten for this condition. These include beet, black sesame, black soybean, caper, dried ginger, Job's tears, turnip, mulberry, and pine nut. The patient should be advised to abstain from foods that cause Dampness, such as goose, peanut, and pineapple. Since Damp Bi syndrome most often affects the knees and since the Kidneys are one of the three organs which govern Liquid in the body (along with the Spleen and Lungs) and also govern the knees, it is often advisable to simultaneously eat some foods that nourish the Kidneys. Finally, since Dampness is a Yin Evil Qi, it is appropriate in general to eat more warming, ascending, and Yang-supporting foods.

See recipes for: Shepherd's Pie with Seitan (Gluten Meat), 122; Ginger Beef or Ginger Seitan "Beef", 122; Baked Mashed Turnips or Daikon Radish, 123; Sauteed (Stir-Fried) Daikon with Scallion and Carrot, 123; Water Chestnut Soup, 124; Gado Gado Sauce, 125; Tuna Stuffed Peppers, 126; Lamb Kidneys Andalusian, 127; Dairyless Pumpkin Pie, 135.

Damp Heat in the Blood of the Foot Jue Yin Meridian

Damp Heat in the Blood of the Foot Jue Yin meridian, the Liver channel, is the most complex of the syndromes we have discussed in this book. When first putting this book together we considered simply giving a diet outline for each syndrome found in introductory texts on Chinese pathology such as *The Web That Has No Weaver*. When our editor reviewed the book he also encouraged this direction. However, it is our clinical experience that the use of dietary therapy is not and should not be as specific as the use of acupuncture or herbs. To set up a dietary protocol mimicking the common format of texts on herbs would be to give a false idea of what diet actually can and cannot do and how it is clinically used by well-practiced by Asian doctors. Such "herbalization" of acupuncture has already become standard in contemporary Traditional Chinese Medicine. Thus we have included only those syndromes in which we feel diet does play a significant part in either their cause or treatment. Elaborate, esoteric dietary regimes to be followed faithfully ingredient for ingredient have been purposely avoided.

However, Damp Heat in the Blood of the Liver meridian is a very intriguing syndrome, all too commonly met, which does merit its own discussion. It is how I most often diagnose Herpes genitalia, the scourge of the so-called sexual revolution. Herpes genitalia is a sexually transmitted, infectious disease. It is characterized by painful skin lesions that are red and hot to the touch. These lesions are generally wet, weeping, and slow to heal. The most common site of these lesions is on or near the genitalia. The fact that they are an infectious disease transmitted by contact classifies them as an External disease. Their painful, hot, weeping nature indicates the invading Evil Qi is Damp and Hot in nature. The area which is attacked is irrigated by the Liver meridian, the Foot Jue Yin. Using the Four Radicals of Hot Disease theory, the invasion has penetrated to the Blood level. Most carbuncles, furuncles, and inflammations of the skin are at the Blood level. Due to Heat the Blood "boils over." Due to this syndrome's resistance to treatment I think we can also posit a strong presence of toxins and because this disease is endemic in our society due to a loosening of sexual morals, I think it can also be classified as a Heavenly Retribution disease.

According to the Theory of Hot Diseases, Heat tends to move down to the Lower Burner. It also tends to associate with Dampness, particularly in the Lower Burner. The Lower Burner is described in Chinese medicine as being like a swamp. It is by nature a poorly circulated area, an area already containing a preponderance of impure or toxic materials (feces, urine, menstrual blood), and an area already damp.

The Kidneys rule the Lower Burner. Kidney vitality is directly responsible for the tonus and defense of the Lower Burner. Weak Kidney energy allows this area to be invaded. During sex the Kidneys are typically, at least temporarily, depleted. This is aggravated by alcohol, drugs, sugar, coffee, emotional stress, masturbation, fatigue and exhaustion, numerous partners, excessive orgasm in the female, and ejaculation in the male. According to Chinese medical theory *vis-a-vis* sexual energetics, all these these things deplete or weaken the Kidneys. All these are also not uncommon components of contemporary sex. Therefore, it is not surprising that today's generation is susceptible to this invasion. In fact, we could qualify our original diagnosis by saying that this Damp Heat invasion is allowed by a Kidney Deficiency, either temporary, for instance after ejaculation, or long-term. One female patient of mine contracted such a Damp Heat invasion while having sex with a man, while another woman sleeping with the same man at the same time did not. In other words, our culture being the way it is, susceptibility to infection depends on immunological resistance, Wei Qi.

In Herpes genitalia this Damp Heat goes through active and latent phases. Clinicians, both western and eastern, have identified a number of factors that seem to trigger the transformation from latent to active. These are stress, fatigue, sex, emotional upset, menstruation, chocolate, sweets, alcohol, coffee, drugs, and nuts. Stress, fatigue, sex, and emotional upset all depress or exhaust the Righteous Qi of the body which is responsible for keeping Evil Qi in check. These factors also specifically deplete Kidney energy. Chocolate, sweets, alcohol, coffee, and drugs also harm and deplete either or both the Middle Burner and the Kidneys, thus depleting the Righteous Qi in general and the Kidney Qi in particular.

In women, the time of menstruation is a time when the energy in general is moving down. In modern women it often does not move down vigorously enough, in part because we are such a "heady" society. Menstruation is also a process of discharging Heat which has accumulated in the Blood due to natural metabolic resons. If anything impairs or hinders a complete discharge of this Heat, it may accumulate or transform with other Heat in the Lower Burner. Due to the emotional turmoil of our contemporary culture, women in general develop an inordinate amount of congestion in their Liver. Take for an example the epidemic of Premenstrual Syndrome which is directly attributable to Liver Qi Congestion. If this adds to a generally stagnant condition in the Lower Burner, it provides a perfect environment for the blossoming of Damp Heat. If this is further complicated by Deficient Blood, that is, if the vigor of the Blood is not up to par, it can easily allow for the flourishing of an Evil Qi. As the heat which is Yang consumes the Blood which is Yin, a loop which is self-perpetuating is created.

Nuts, interestingly, are a food contraindicated in Liver disorders due to their oiliness and indigestibility. Their role in aggravating Herpes is probably attributable to the Liver's role in this scenario. Although the Liver meridian is not the same as the Liver organ, if the organ becomes imbalanced this will tend to aggravate any pathological changes along the course of its associated meridian.

The logical treatment principles are to cool the Heat in the Blood, dry the Damp, nourish the Blood, relax the Liver, circulate the Lower Burner, and tonify the Kidneys. During active phases the Evil Qi should be attacked forcefully. More attention should be given to cooling the Heat in the Blood and drying Damp. During latent phases more attention should be given to relaxing the Liver, nourishing the Blood and tonifying the Kidneys. I do not know if it is possible to claim a cure once a person has been positively infected by Herpes genitalia. I am certain from clinical experience that by following these treatment principles the frequency, severity, and duration of Herpes outbreaks can definitely be reduced. In many cases, the remission or latency seems indefinite, but only time will tell.

Not all these issues are totally or specifically related to diet. As we have seen, the causative factors are complex. However, diet is definitely important during the active phase. Foods such as shrimp, trout, and mustard greens that aggravate Heat in the Blood should be avoided, and foods that cool Heat in Blood should be eaten, such as black fungus, butter, cheese, gluten, and peppermint. During the latent phase, a tonifying diet should be adopted, staying away from foods and drugs that either deplete the Middle Burner, the Postnatal Qi, or the Kidneys, the Prenatal Qi. Such a diet has already been well outlined. In addition, for women or men with Blood Deficiency, special care should be taken to include Blood tonifying and nourishing foods in the diet. These include amasake, raspberry, pork, rice, pear, longan, lotus root, kidney bean, winter squash, fig, coconut milk, and chestnut.

Diet alone is usually not enough to keep Herpes under control. Lifestyle and sexual relations must also be adjusted to decrease stress and drain on the Kidneys. In a total treatment plan, acupuncture and Chinese herbal formulae play important parts. Herbs are used to maintain the constitutional vigor and acupuncture is effective in reducing pain and inflammation and to speed healing in the treatment of acute outbreaks.

Half-Truths and Misconceptions

A number of half-truths and misconceptions exist within the alternative health care community about certain foods. These beliefs lead to excessively rigid diets or to altogether erroneous diets. Amongst health food advocates today the most commonly misunderstood foods are sugar, salt, red meat, milk and milk products, wheat, and so-called nightshade family vegetables.

Almost everyone knows that "sugar is bad for you." But sugar is not bad for you. It is the amount which we consume that is deleterious. It is unhealthy to eat too much sugar. It is equally unhealthy to fanatically avoid everything that includes sugar. In small amounts, or in certain situations, a little sugar is very beneficial, even medicinal. In fact, I believe sugar should be viewed as a powerful medicine. Sugar is very tonifying to the Stomach and Spleen. It tonifies Qi and Blood and it produces Fluid. The sweet flavor is tonifying in general but refined sugar is excessively sweet.

For the average person in good health, sugar is too sweet. Its excessive sweetness is unnecessary. Instead of strengthening the digestion it has the opposite effect. According to Five Element Theory, too much of any flavor harms the organs associated with that flavor. Sugar first weakens the Middle Burner Fire by smothering that Fire in an over-production of Fluid which then accumulates in the Spleen and Stomach. This causes Damp Spleen. Eventually, through the Control cycle and through the special relationship of Middle

Burner to the Kidney Fire, Kidney Yang energy is also exhausted. Sugar also has a strong ascending nature and overconsumption will lead to too much energy rising to the upper half of the body creating an Excess there while leaving the lower half Deficient. This may manifest as mucous disorders, hyperactivity, fluid accumulation disorders, fatigue, and emotional disorders, all of which are common in our culture.

On the other hand, in Deficient Fluid or Dry syndromes a little sugar is appropriate. It is also appropriate in Stomach and Spleen Deficiency syndromes in which Dampness and Water Toxin are not a part. Cough syrups made with a sugar base are therefore very appropriate for Dry Lung cough or Yin Deficiency of the Lungs. This endorsement of sugar as a legitimate medicinal food is not meant as encouragement to "pig out" on junk food. It is meant to put sugar in a perspective so that a decision to eat sugar is based on a more complete energetic description of its nature. From the classical Chinese medical point of view, sugar is not a Yin food. It is a Yang food of which overconsumption will produce a Yin imbalance, over-production of Fluid in the Middle Burner.

To many middle-aged and older Americans salt is an anathema since it can contribute to high blood pressure. To Macrobiotics, salt is very beneficial since it is very "Yang" and most disease is a "Yin" process. Both of these views of salt are simplistic. Salt, like sugar, is a very strong medicinal food. Its consumption can be either very good or very bad. Whether it is good or bad depends upon the individual situation and even this may change over a period of time. According to Chinese medicine salt is cold; it is very salty; it lowers the energy; it also lubricates Dryness, particularly in the lower abdomen; it softens hard accumulations; and it cools the Blood. It is not Yang according to Chinese medicine, but Yin.

Salt's flavor is *excessively salty*. According to Five Element Theory, it does not take much salt to weaken the Kidneys. A little salt can help to tonify the Kidney Yin and to lower or center the Qi in the lower or root half of the body. If the root is solid, it will anchor the Qi. However, in cases of hypertension it is important to avoid salt or to use it very carefully, since almost all hypertension results from a weakening of the Kidneys which allows the Liver energy to rise out of control. In such cases salt only exacerbates the situation. Instead, Kidney tonifying foods such as Kidney organ meat may be used, but not salt itself.

According to the classics, overconsumption of salt will also cause the pulse to become sluggish, indicating Qi congestion. The complexion will lose its vitality, the Blood will be harmed, the bones will become weak, and the muscles and flesh will wither as the Jing or Essence is weakened. The functions of the Heart will be suppresssed because the Little Fire of the Lower Burner will not be able to support the Big Fire of the Heart. This scenario is not uncommon among Macrobiotics whose emaciation, low spirits, fragile quality, and darkish complexions all show signs of overconsumption of salt.

Salt should not be thought of as a balance to sugar. Both foods have their own qualities and natures. Each food should be eaten or avoided based on the merits of its individual qualities and how those qualities match in principle the symptoms and signs of the situation. In our list of the attributes and uses of salt according to Chinese medicine, most of the actual methods of employing it therapeutically are topical rather than internal. Moxa is burned on top of salt for abdominal pain and swelling due to Middle Burner Deficiency. Salt is used to brush the teeth in pyorrhea. Salt water is gargled for sore throat and salt poultices are used in skin eruptions. Again, only familiarity with clinical practice can really elucidate the therapeutic principles listed in a book.

So, a little salt is beneficial for the average person. In the winter its moderate use can help to lower the Qi and to tonify the Yin of the Kidneys. In the summer it can help to cool the body as in the use of salt tablets by athletes. However, individuals with edema, hypertension, or Kidney or Heart problems should only use salt as directed by a competent physician. Its use should be energetically enlightened and not based on the hazy concept of balancing it against sugar.

Like salt and sugar, red meat has fallen into disfavor with many Americans. The eating of meat, red or otherwise, is considered unethical both socio-politically and spiritually. We should keep our meat consumption to a minimum, but as discussed in the section on the Doctrine of Signatures, a complete and abrupt cessation of meat-eating can cause long term problems if other, higher sources of energy are not ingested.

Meat is very tonifying to both the Qi and Blood. It is also difficult to digest. Eating too much meat usually produces Dampness accumulating in the Spleen (since the flavor of meat is sweet) and contributes to the accumulation of Glairy Mucous, since its components are often not fully metabolized. In addition, the high fat content and high percentage of "impure energies" or waste products in meat stress or aggravate the Liver/Gallbladder. When meat is eaten, it should be taken in very small quantities and in soups or broths. For many Deficiency syndromes it is difficult to quickly and adequately tonify the Qi and particularly difficult to tonify the Blood if small quantities of meat are not included in the diet. Even in Chinese herbal medicine, animal "herbs" are commonly employed to tonify the internal organs, Blood, and Jing. Meat is most appropriately eaten in the Fall and Winter when more tonifying foods generally should be eaten.

Milk and milk products have also fallen out of favor among the health conscious. Some Americans eschew any and all milk products because they are "mucous forming." However humans have eaten milk for millenia and until recently milk has always been regarded as highly nutritious and healthful. To discriminate who, when, and how much milk one should eat one must first understand the energetic nature of milk. According to Chinese medicine milk is neutral, sweet, ascending, travels to the Lungs, Stomach, and Heart, is Yang and pertains to the Earth Element. In principle milk is tonifying in Deficiency, tonifies Qi and Blood, produces Fluid, and lubricates the intestines. Medicinally, it is used in the treatment of indigestion, diabetes, and constipation. It is contraindicated in Middle Burner Deficiency, Dampness, and Sputum.

Thus, milk is a little hard to digest and if eaten to excess or consumed by a person with weak digestion it can produce Sputum. This tendency to produce Sputum is particularly prevalent in pasteurized and homogenized milk products that are "wrecked" or dead. Such milk is rendered deficient of the Fire of Life and therefore requires too much Middle Burner Fire to digest completely. Milk products that have not been pasteurized or homogenized do not create as much Sputum. Also milk products that are predigested and alive such as yogurt are also not as mucous-producing. Milk products are very therapeutic for patients suffering from a Deficiency of Yin with Internal Fire causing emaciation, loss of weight, constipation, and dry skin. Only people whose digestive Fire is weak and who produce mucous easily need to stay away from milk. Otherwise, there is no need to be fanatical in avoiding milk.

Many Americans complain of being allergic to wheat. Wheat's energy is cool. Wheat clears Heat, tones the Blood, calms the Spirit/Mind, and tones the Kidneys. Its directional energy is descending. Amongst those whose Middle Burner Fire is Deficient, wheat may also be hard to digest. This, as in the case of milk, is particularly true when wheat products are dead or wrecked as is white bread filled with preservatives. Wheat products are not so cooling and are more easily digested if the wheat is whole, freshly ground, thoroughly cooked, and eaten with other foods that are warming and easily digestible.

The fact that we in America eat so much wheat seems appropriate since our culture's energy is so ascending, we are so frenetic, and our Kidneys and Heart are so stressed. We middle-aged and younger Americans are so depleted by Excessive lifestyle that our Fire is Deficient, rendering us less capable of digesting such foods as wheat. This is a dangerous trend and does not bode well for the future if it continues. Pure Excess syndromes are relatively easy and straightforward to treat but mixed Excess/Deficiency syndromes are much more complicated. Wheat that is properly prepared, well cooked, and combined with appropriate foods can help keep us from "burning out."

Many health food writers refer to tomatoes, potatoes, and eggplant as the nightshade family of vegetables. It is true that these three vegetables do belong to the same botanical family as belladonna, the "deadly nightshade." This does not mean, however, that these vegetables are also deadly or even minor poisons. Even belladonna reveals its medicinal use to those who can view things from a larger perspective. Overconsumption of eggplant may harm the uterus since it activates the Qi and Blood of that region without doing much to tonify them. However, in cases of Stagnant Blood of the Lower Burner (one common etiology of chronic venereal infections, PID, ovarian cysts, uterine myomas, dysmenorrhea, and amenorrhea), the Qi and Blood activating and Stagnant Blood removing qualities of eggplant are highly desirable.

Potato is one of the few vegetable foods that tonify the Kidney Yin. As such it is an important Winter food. Potato tonifies Deficiency in general and tonifies the Spleen in particular. In Chinese medicine potato is not considered toxic.

Tomato clears Heat and produces Fluid. Its energetic nature is cool and descending. It strengthens the Stomach. Its flavor is both sweet and sour and its element ascription is to both Earth and Wood. In the Summer it is useful for counteracting Summer Heat. In the Fall it combats a tendency to Dryness. In general it can help harmonize the Liver and the Stomach. It is appropriate to eat tomato raw in the Summer, but in the Fall it should be cooked. Like any and every other food it should not be eaten excessively or exclusively but it does have its use.

Patient Acceptance

One of the biggest problems with the majority of dietary therapies is that they are so extreme or so unappetizing that patients refuse to follow them. Many patients who have been placed on restrictive diets say they would rather eat well and die early than be deprived of delicious food. One well-known Macrobiotic dietary counselor told me that his diets help eighty percent of his patients but that only forty percent or less stay on his diets long enough to get results. Eighty percent of forty percent is only a little better than thirty percent and thirty percent is not a very good amelioration rate. Therapy that is unacceptable to the patient is not wise therapy no matter how sound its other principles may be. The best diet in the world is meaningless if the patient won't stay on it.

It is my experience that when I suggest to patients they should eat mostly cooked vegetables, some whole grains, some small amounts of meat, little or no raw fruits and vegetables, and no cold or iced foods, they often tell me such a diet is boring. However, it is not the foods themselves that are boring but the uninspired way many Americans prepare these foods. A great deal of contemporary disease is a product of our over-complex, over-exciting lifestyle. In general I believe that the diet as well as the lifestyle should be fairly simple. I also believe that such simplicity should be thoughtful, artistic, and tasteful. In addition, it is my experience that the only change which is healthy and enduring is that which evolves from within over a long period of time and not radical change imposed from without. Therefore, in the following sections my wife and I have suggested a number of recipes which may seem to some proponents of more spartan regimes more like gourmet fare than remedial recipes.

74

However, all these recipes are based on the sound dietary principles of classical Chinese medicine and at least half have been employed clinically in China for generations. The Macrobiotic therapist referred to previously told me that since it is very hard to get people to modify their diets the Chinese had given up on dietary therapy as a waste of time. This is patently not the case. It is just that his extremism could not even perceive Chinese dietary therapy. Patients thrive only if they both believe in and enthusiastically embrace their therapy.

Diet and Exercise

Diet is only one of the factors that contribute to health and long life. Any therapy or health care system which is limited to a single modality cannot be considered holistic nor will it be effective. Health is a function of living in accord with the larger flow of the Universe, spiritually, mentally, emotionally, and physically. Life is more than just eating. As Ko Hung wrote in the 4th Century C.E.:

"In everything pertaining to the nurturing of life one must learn much and make the essentials one's own; look widely and know how to select. There should be no reliance upon only one particular speciality, for there is always the danger that breadwinners will emphasize their own specialities. That is why those who know recipes for sexual intercourse say that only these recipes can lead to Fullness of Life. Those who know breathing procedures claim that only circulation of the breaths can prolong our years. Those knowing methods of bending and stretching say only calisthenics can exorcise old age. Those knowing herbal prescriptions say that only through the nibbling of medicines can one be free from exhaustion. Failures in the study of the divine process are due to such specializations. People with shallow experience who happen to know one particular thing well will immediately declare it a panacea."[17]

In particular, diet must be juxtaposed with exercise or physical activity. What we eat provides the material fuel and substrate of our incarnation. What we do is the functional activity of our organism.

Even if we eat the most expensive, exotic, and healthful foods but fail to exercise, we will not and cannot be healthy.

"Lack of physical exercise or necessary physical exertion may cause retardation of circulation of Qi and Blood, general weaknesss, lassitude, obesity, and shortness of breath after exertion. It may also lower the general resistance of the body."[18]

If the body's Fires become weak, food will not be completely metabolized and the residue will become toxic agents such as Glairy Mucous. On the other hand, a system in good working order, full of vigor and the activity of life, will tend to burn off more impurities in the diet than will a sedentary one. We all know of healthy, active, and energetic individuals who work hard daily and who eat alot of junk food. The less active we become, the more careful we must also be with what we eat. However, this may lead to an unhealthy fixation on food which can then lead to further organic and emotional imbalances. Exercise is the Yang to diet's Yin and the two must always be practiced together.

Cancer and Chinese Dietary Therapy

For modern Americans cancer is perhaps the scariest disease. It can affect anyone at any age, its prognosis is poor and heroic allopathic treatments such as surgery, radiation, and chemotherapy are as mutilating as the disease they seek to cure. The diagnosis of cancer is received as the kiss of Death. Since the general public is dubious about allopathic cancer cures, many cancer patients seek alternative treatments such as Laetrile, "black poultices," the Kelly diet, the Gerson diet, or the Macrobiotic diet. In fact, the majority of alternative treatments for cancer center around or include a specific dietary regime.

Almost without exception these diets are based on one or several specific foods or an exclusive approach, such as raw foods, vegetarianism, or fasting. Each approach cites testimonials of its empirical success. However, not one of these diets can comprehensively "cure" cancer. From the Chinese medical point of view, this is because there is no single "cancer" disease. In Chinese medicine a number of different energetic diagnoses are used to explain the various symptoms and syndromes which western physicians call cancer. Although the formation of a tumor or neoplasm is always described as a local stagnation/accumulation of one sort or another, the underlying cause of such stagnation may be one of many Chinese energetic etiologies. Therefore, in Chinese medicine there is and can be no single cancer-curing diet.

Two patients diagnosed by western medicine as having cancer may be given two entirely different dietary therapies by a Chinese clinician. If the patient is generally Excessive, a technical Chinese medical term which should not be taken out of context, the diet plan will be generally dispersive or eliminative. Foods that are cleansing will be emphasized. If a patient is basically Deficient, such a cleansing diet would only speed their degeneration and demise. Such patients must be fed a nourishing and building diet. Often Excess and Deficiency are present in a complicated interrelationship. In such cases the diet must also be carefully balanced in terms of the specific energetic diagnosis.

Chinese medicine emphasizes two factors which must always be kept in mind. One is the Righteous Qi or healthy energy of the person. The other is the Evil Qi or pathogenic energy. Western medicine places all its emphasis on fighting and negating the Evil or pathogenic energy. Chinese medicine also fights the Evil Qi, but takes into account the status of the Righteous Qi. If the Righteous Qi becomes debilitated so that vital bodily functions are impaired, the first duty is to restore and support the Righteous Qi. The active battle against the Evil Qi is de-emphasized until the person has recuperated their strength.

Not only does Western medicine not understand nor emphasize the role of Righteous Qi but most contemporary dietary cancer cures also do not pay enough attention to the support of the Righteous Qi. In general many, if not most, "cancer diets" are eliminative diets which seek to purge or purify the body of the Evil Qi, the cancer. With seriously debilitated patients such a course of treatment will only hasten their demise. This is not only theory. It has been my personal experience and observation. Three of my friends who stuck to an erroneous dietary treatment plan are dead because of that mistake.

Any dietary plan for the treatment of cancer which is not based on an individual and specific energetic diagnosis is likely to lead a patient into the same trap. Such oversimplification shows a lack of knowledge and wisdom regarding disease and the body's functions. It also belies the fact that the modern medical model with its oversimplification and extremes underlies even the majority of "natural" alternative therapies.

Although a proper dietary treatment plan based on an individual and specific diagnosis is a must in the treatment of the complex and deeply-rooted energetic syndromes identified as cancer, such dietary treatment should not be the sole or even the most important part of the overall treatment plan. Herbal formulae supported by other appropriate modalities such as acupuncture, massage, and spa therapy are the foundation of the traditional Chinese medical treatment of cancer.

The energetic syndromes which manifest as cancer are all serious and advanced patterns of disharmony. They are not light, superficial or easy to cure. In Chinese medicine the prognosis is also often poor. Sometimes Chinese medicine can treat cancers which western medicine cannot due to its generally superior conceptualization of the organism. More often, a combination of western heroic measures plus Chinese holistic methods proves most successful. However there are no easy answers to the problem of cancer since it underscores the degeneracy of our environment, our diets, lifestyles, morals, and mental states. It is the product of an erroneous relationship with reality. It is the expression of this Kali Yuga on the level of health and disease.

The Doctrine of Signatures

Chinese medicine is a cosmological system. It is based on cosmic principles of growth, change, and development. These principles are universal and can be applied to all levels and aspects of reality. It must be noted that they are not reality itself but only our conceptualization of reality and are true only by virtue of their pragmatic value. Because everything manifests according to these principles, things that look similar or share similar structures embody similar principles. Their growth is due to similar energies. In all traditional cultures based on a magical/mystical insight which arises from altered states of consciousness induced by yogic practices, there is a concept of what in Medieval times was called the Doctrine of Signatures. According to this perception of reality, a root that looks like a man, Ginseng, "man root," is a tonic for the whole human being. Oysters, which look like testes, are believed to be tonifying to the human sexual energies, particularly the male or Yang energies. Rocky Mountain Oysters, traditionally beef and sheep testes and now turkey as well, are even more effective for this purpose than actual oysters. Another way of stating the Doctrine of Signatures is "Like cures like." Chinese medicine takes this principle for granted; for example, in the 6th Century C.E. Sun Sze Mo prescribed organ meats as a dietary cure for diseases of those same organs, particularly Deficiency states.

In my clinical experience, I find organ meats to be very effective therapeutically. I often recommend Kidneys to people with Kidney Deficiencies, Liver for Liver Yin or Liver Blood Deficiencies, and oysters and Rocky Mountain Oysters for sexual Deficiencies. These foods are not commonly eaten by most Americans. When they are useful for a given individual, the physician should point out their medical effect and their low price as well as providing hints and recipes for their preparation. A number of recipes for Liver and Kidneys are included in this book.

If possible, such meats should be purchased from health food stores which carry "clean" and organic meats. Some patients fear that these organs may have accumulated toxins from the environment. It is my feeling that the beneficial effects of organ meats, used infrequently and in small, medicinal amounts outweigh any presumed danger of accumulated toxins. If the individual's organs are functioning well and in a balanced way, they are better able to filter and discharge all types of toxins. A weak, malfunctioning system creates toxic wastes out of even the best quality, organically produced foods.

When using organ or any other meats, one should give some thought to the ethical issues implied. A sentient being has to be killed in order for us to eat their flesh. Everyone who participates in the murder of another sentient being also reaps the karmic result of physical suffering. In order to minimize this contradictory result, it is my belief that one should not purposefully kill an animal for its flesh or organs unless the patient's very life is threatened. Even then the patient should perform various expiatory practices and work for the spiritual welfare of that sentient being's subsequent rebirths. A debt of gratitude and a karmic responsibility should be acknowledged. If one does not ordinarily eat meat and finds that organs are available in the market from already slaughtered animals, one should look upon those organs as being a gift from the universe, a manifestation of appropriateness or the ripening of past good karma. Even so, one should acknowledge gratitude for the animal whose body is eaten and work for its future benefit.

The great Taoist saint and Chinese doctor, Tao Hung-Ching, compiled a pharmacopoeia in which he recommended using many animal organs and by-products. After practicing yogic austerities for many years he failed to attain Immortality, although one of his students did. He asked his student why he had attained the rank of a Celestial before his Teacher, since this is not the normal order of such things. Since the student was an Immortal he agreed to fly to Heaven to ask the Jade Emperor why his esteemed Teacher, Tao Hung-Ching, had not achieved Immortality before him. The Jade Emperor responded that since Tao Hung-Ching had recommended the slaughter of so many animals, it was impossible for him to pass beyond the bounds of karma. When the disciple returned to Earth and told Tao Hung-Ching this, Tao Hung-Ching sat down and crossed out all the formulae recommending the use of animal parts which were not absolutely life saving. Having done this he also eventually became a Celestial.

An important contraindication in the use of organ meats should be mentioned. Some westerners misinterpreting the Five Element Theory advocate eating Liver in the Spring as a way of helping the Liver in its corresponding season. According to the great Chang Chung-Ching in his *Chin Kuei Yao Lueh*, this is a mistake.

"In spring liver should not be eaten; in summer heart should not be eaten; in autumn lung should not be eaten; in winter

80

kidney should not be eaten; in all seasons spleen should not be eaten. The reasons for these prohibitions are several. In spring the liver reaches its climax of exuberance and depletes the spleen. The eating of liver augments the exuberance and further depletes the spleen, ultimately leading to an incurable condition. Also, during the liver's exuberant period, the genuine hepatic Ch'i should not be introduced into the liver, otherwise the soul will be injured. In all except the exuberant season, it is good to supplement the liver with liver. This rule applies to other visceral organs as well."[19]

I myself have had the opportunity to verify Chang's opinion. Recently, a patient of mine, suffering from Liver Qi Constraint manifesting as dysmenorrhea, took Liver extract pills in the Spring thinking this might help her condition. It resulted in a facial tic around the eyes which disappeared as soon as the Liver extract was discontinued.

I would however disagree with Chang Chung-Ching, if I dare to be so presumptuous, vis-a-vis eating Kidneys in the Winter. According to the famous Dr. Chu Dan-Xi, the Yin tends to be Deficient. Based on this principle and Dr. Chang Ching-Yue's principle of tonifying the Prenatal Qi, the Kidneys, I do suggest eating Kidneys in the Winter in any case where there is Kidney Deficiency. With only rare exception, the Kidneys cannot have too much energy. This is an example of how the theories of classical Chinese medicine have been expanded and refined over the centuries.

Congee
and
Chinese Casserole Cooking

Although it is not our intention to suggest that Americans must eat Chinese food in order to be healthy, there are two styles of cooking practiced in China which we believe do merit inclusion in the American diet. One we term Congee and the other Chinese Casserole Cooking.

Congee is an Anglo-Indian word which means rice gruel or porridge. In Chinese it is called Shi-fan or "water rice." As the name implies, it is a thin rice soup, the basis of which is rice and water. This incredibly simple food has a number of health benefits. It is easy to digest and assimilate, it tonifies both Qi and Blood, it tones and harmonizes the Middle Burner, and it promotes urination. Depending on what is cooked with the Congee, it can have almost unlimited medicinal applications. Lord Buddha considered Congee made with milk and honey to be the chief medicinal food for preserving health. In the *Mahavagga* of the *Vinaya Pitaka*, Lord Buddha is recorded as saying:

It confers ten things on him: life and beauty, ease and strength; It dispels hunger, thirst, and wind; It cleanses the bladder, It digests food. This medicine is praised by the Wellfarer.[20]

In much of China, Congee is eaten as a breakfast food. It is served plain although it is accompanied by various side dishes including hard-boiled preserved eggs, pickles, steamed buns, and dried shredded fish. In southern China Congee takes on the status of a one-pot meal. A varying number and combination of ingredients may be added to this rice soup depending upon one's desire or its intended therapeutic use. Below are a number of foods which can be added to rice Congee and their specific effects. These are based on a list which appears in the English synopsis of Li Shih-Zhen's *Pen-tsao Kang-mu*.[21] These have also been suggested by Da Liu in his book *The Tao of Health and Longevity*.

Wheat Congee	Cooling, a febrifuge; also calming and sedating due to wheat's nourishing effect on the Heart
Apricot Kernel Congee	Good for cough and asthma; expels sputum
Sweet Rice Congee	Tones Middle Burner; tonifies Qi; digestant and tonic in Deficiency diarrhea, vomiting, indigestion, etc.
Mung Bean Congee	Cooling, febrifuge; specially cools Summer Heat
Aduki Bean Congee	Removes Damp; useful in edema and gout; also useful in retention of urine, oliguria, dysuria, and other Kidney/Bladder problems
Water Chestnut Congee	Cooling to viscera; good for Excess diabetes and jaundice
Chestnut Congee	Tonifies Kidneys, strengthens lower back and knees; also useful in treating anal hemorrhage
Taro Congee	Nutritive and tonifying
Radish Congee	Digestant; cools Hot problems of digestive organs
Carrot Congee	Carminative and peptic; good for indigestion and chronic dysentery; antitussive
Purslane Congee	Detoxifying; possibly useful for herpes genitalia
Spinach Congee	Harmonizing and moistening to viscera; sedative; lowers Rebellious Qi
Shepherd's Purse Congee	Sharpens vision and benefits Liver
Celery Congee	Cooling and hypotensive in early stages of Liver Yang Ascension
Leek Congee	Warming and tonifying; good for chronic diarrhea
Pinenut Congee	Moistens Heart and Lungs; harmonizes Large Intestine; useful in Wind diseases and constipation

Scallion Bulb Congee	Cures Cold Diarrhea in the elderly
Dry Ginger Congee	Deficiency and Cold digestive problems such as diarrhea, anorexia, vomiting, and indigestion
Fennel Congee	Carminative; cures Qi Stagnation hernia
Kidney Congee	Generally tonifying, specially to Kidneys; useful in Deficiency symptoms such as impotence, spermatorrhea, Deficiency lumbago, weak knees, premature ejaculation.
Liver Congee	Deficiency diseases of the Liver as in Liver Blood or Liver Yin Deficiency; also good in Kidney Yin Deficiency

The possibilities of creating remedial and therapeutic Congees are almost limitless. Medicinal herbs can be added during cooking and removed before eating. Several foods which have different therapeutic actions can be mixed together to achieve a combined effect similar to an herbal formula. Chinese herbs that are sometimes decocted in Congees include Rehmannia, Deer Antler, Lycium, and Poria. Some people strain the liquid from the congee and just drink this instead of eating the porridge. This is recommended when Congee is being used as a supplement to mother's milk for infants or in treatment of seriously ill and weakened patients.

One of my favorite breakfast Congees is made with Chinese red dates and fresh sliced ginger sweetened with a little honey. Red dates are a sedative and calm the Spirit. They are also strengthening to the digestion. Ginger promotes circulation of Qi and Blood, assists the Yang and warms the Middle Burner. Honey nourishes the Heart, calms the Spirit and lubricates the Intestines. To this, I often add walnuts to tonify the Kidney Yang and nourish the brain, and chestnuts to tonify the Kidney Yin and strengthen the Jing.

Since rice is a diuretic, Congee is contraindicated in Deficiency polyuria and nocturia. Congee eaten by patients with a tendency to polyuria due to Kidney Qi Deficiency or Kidney Yang Deficiency will experience an aggravation of their symptoms. If this continues it will result in terminal dribbling and a sensation of retained urine which are signs of further Deficiency.

In some cases Congee is an integral part of the herbal therapy. When using Cinnamon Formula as a diaphoretic in the treatment of the initial stage of the common cold in a patient of weak conformation, Congee should be eaten after the ingestion of the herbal decoction in order to achieve the desired effect. In *Shang Han Lun*, Chang Chung-Ching writing on the administration of Cinnamon Formula says, "Wait for a short time ⟨ after having taken the herbal decoction ⟩ and then take one or more Sheng of hot congee to institute a joint action."[22] Zhou Feng-Wu explains the use of Congee as an adjunct to Cinnamon Formula in an article entitled "The Indications of Decoction Ramulus Cinnamomi Composite:"

"The administration of hot dilute porridge aids the Stomach Qi, provides substance for the Ying and Wei, benefits the fluid, assists the distribution of the fluid of the Middle Warmer, and carries the hidden evil with the sweet towards the surface. It is to be noted that the drinking of hot dilute porridge is one of the essential components of the Decoction Ramulus Cinnamomi Composite."[23]

Our method of making Congee is as follows. Place one part rice per five to six parts water in a heavy, lidded pot. The amount of water will determine how thick the porridge will be. Place the pot on Warm if using an electric stove or hot plate, or on the lowest flame possible if using a gas range. Let simmer four to six hours. If the Congee is to be eaten for breakfast, start it just before retiring for bed the night before. Upon rising be sure to stir the pot so the Congee will not burn on the bottom. It can be reheated during the day. Crockpots are very useful for cooking Congee. Leftover Congee can be added to bread dough. The yeast will quicken it so it should not be regarded as Wrecked.

At the Great Wall Restaurant at 815 Washington Street in San Francisco's Chinatown, one can order from a selection of various multi-ingredient Congees. The first time we ate there the waiter said we wouldn't want the Congee, that it was just for Chinese people. He was reluctant to serve it to us then, but a year later there was no such difficulty and we noticed a number of "Anglos" eating in this restaurant which specializes in Congee and Chinese Casserole Cooking. The Eight Treasure Congee is particularly good. It contains peas, shrimp, squid, liver, chicken gizzards and whatever else the chef chooses for that day. In general it is an excellent meal for tonifying the Kidneys, Liver, and Middle Burner, and for calming the Spirit.

The second Chinese style of cooking which is very healthful and relatively unknown here in the United States is Chinese Casserole Cooking which is also called "family-style cooking." Like Congee it is a one-pot meal. Also like Congee, its forte is that it does not require alot of cooking oil. This style of cooking requires relatively little energy and maintains the fresh food values and flavors of the ingredients. Depending upon the ingredients, one can create a one-pot meal therapeutic for almost any syndrome, although this style does lend itself more to the preparation of meals which tonify Deficiency.

Chinese Casserole Cooking was called *Keng* in antiquity.[24] It was the dominant method of food preparation from the Chou dynasty (1124-249 BC) up through the Han dynasty (206 BC-220 AD). Clay Pot Cooking is another name for this style. Since fuel is expensive in such a densely populated country as China, ovens are not common and oven baking is used infrequently as a cooking method. This style of cooking is done on the stove top, creating a miniature oven within the clay pot. It requires a lidded clay pot, but any heavy ceramic casserole with a cover will do. Romertopfs, the popular German casseroles, work very well and are what we use. However, special clay pots are available in hardware and cooking supply stores in larger Chinatowns across the country.

The recipes below are adapted from Lilah Kan's book *Introducing Chinese Casserole Cookery*. Those interested in this style of cooking should refer to that book for further excellent recipes. The Great Wall Restaurant mentioned above also specializes in clay pot cooking.

Oyster-Walnut Casserole   Serves 4

This recipe is good for tonifying the Kidneys if they are either Yin or Yang Deficient. It is also beneficial to the Lungs and Large Intestine. It is good for Dry Yin Deficient Lungs when no Sputum is present.

15 (ore more) DRIED OYSTERS

1 lb. CHINESE or ITALIAN SWEET SAUSAGE

1 dozen DRIED CHINESE BLACK MUSHROOMS

1 can SLICED WATER CHESTNUTS

1 can SLICED BAMBOO SHOOTS

1 cup PEAS (fresh or frozen)

1 cup CHOPPED WALNUTS

Marinade

4 tsp. SOY SAUCE or TAMARI

4 tsp. COOKING SHERRY

½ tsp. SUGAR

½ tsp. SESAME OIL

¼ tsp. FINELY GRATED GINGER ROOT

Braising Liquid

2 tsp. SOY SAUCE

1 T. COOKING SHERRY

½ tsp. SUGAR

½ cup OYSTER-SOAKING LIQUID (reserved)

2 T. OYSTER SAUCE

Soak oysters in water for 24 hours, changing the water twice. Drain, reserving the water from the final soak. Chop into ½ inch pieces.

Mix the marinade for the sausage. Chop the sausage into ½ pieces and marinate for 1 hour.

Soak the dried mushrooms in water for 1 hour. Drain, remove stems and dice into small slivers. Drain water chestnuts and bamboo shoots and chop to the right size. Measure the peas and walnuts.

Put your wok on high heat and add about 1½ T. of peanut or sesame oil. Tilt the wok to coat all sides. When hot, add oysters, mushrooms and drained marinated sausage. Saute for a few minutes over medium heat until the sausage is well browned, stirring frequently.

Mix the braising ingredients in a 2-quart heavy lidded casserole or dutch oven. Add the cooked mixture to the pot. Bring to a boil; then reduce heat to medium-low, cover, and cook for 15 minutes. Then add the water chestnuts, bamboo shoots, peas, and walnuts. Cover casserole and simmer for another 15 minutes.

To bind the mixture add 2 tsp. cornstarch mixed in 2 tsp. water and stir well, until it is all slightly thickened.

Serve the stew hot over noodles, rice, or on a bed of fresh lettuce.

Lord Buddha's Delight Casserole   Serves 2

This casserole may include many things, depending upon what you have on hand or what strikes your mood. The water chestnuts, gluten, and mushrooms make this version of the dish an excellent tonic for Hyper Liver Yang. In order not to harm the Kidneys, make sure the bean curd is well cooked; fry it on all sides very slowly and for a long time *before* it goes into the casserole.

6 DRIED BLACK CHINESE MUSHROOMS
6 CLOUD EAR TREE MUSHROOMS
12 DRIED DAY LILY PODS
½ lb. FIRM TOFU
½ can SLICED WATER CHESTNUTS
½ can SLICED BAMBOO SHOOTS
1 10-oz. can BRAISED GLUTEN or SEITAN
¼ lb. CHOPPED SNOW PEAS or CHOPPED BROCCOLI

Braising Liquid

2 T. SOY SAUCE or TAMARI

4 T. SHERRY

1 tsp. HONEY or SUGAR

½ cup MUSHROOM-SOAKING LIQUID

½ cup WATER or VEGETABLE STOCK

Cover the mushrooms with warm water and soak for 1 hour. Drain, reserving the liquid. Remove and discard the stems. Cut the caps into quarters. Soak the cloud ears for ½ hour; drain. Soak the day lilies for ½ hour; drain.

Line a large lidded casserole with fresh lettuce leaves. Put all the ingredients except snow peas and tofu on top.

Cut the tofu into cubes and set aside.

Mix braising liquid ingredients well; pour the liquid over the casserole. Bring the liquid to a boil over high heat. Reduce to medium low, cover and simmer for 30 minutes.

While it is simmering, fry the tofu cubes over medium heat on all six sides until quite brown.

After 30 minutes, add the broccoli if you are using it and simmer another 10 minutes. If using snow peas, simmer for 5 more minutes. Add the tofu cubes at the same time. If using broccoli, check after 10 minutes to see if you like the broccoli at that level of crunchiness; if not, simmer a few minutes longer.

Drizzle a bit of roasted sesame oil over the casserole and serve hot over rice or with Chinese noodles.

This recipe takes one hour of soaking time, 15 minutes to assemble, 40 minutes to cook and serves 2 people as a main course, 4 to 5 as part of a larger meal.

Spicy Chicken Gizzards and Hearts   Serves 4

This recipe is a tonification treatment. It has the surprising quality of tasting European rather than Chinese. It is excellent for the digestion and as a tonic for Kidney Yin Deficiency. It is also an appropriate meal for postpartum recuperation and is quite inexpensive.

SESAME OIL (for browning meat and onions)

1 lb. CHICKEN GIZZARDS AND HEARTS (trimmed of fat; gizzards cut in half)

1 ONION (medium to large; chopped in ¼-inch moon slices)

2 POTATOES (good size; chopped in inch-sized cubes)

2 LARGE CARROTS (sliced in ½-inch diagonals)

½ lb. CUT FRESH GREEN BEANS or 2 ribs CHOPPED CELERY or ½ head CHOPPED CABBAGE

Sauce

¼ cup COOKING SHERRY

½ tsp. HONEY or SUGAR

½ tsp. 5-SPICE POWDER

2 CLOVES MASHED GARLIC (or more to taste)

1 one-eighth inch SLICE FRESH GINGER ROOT (flattened)

8 oz. can TOMATO SAUCE

Cook the meat and onion in a hot wok with sesame oil, until the onion is translucent and the meat is beginning to brown. Stir constantly.

Mix all sauce ingredients in a large heavy casserole. Add all the ingredients and mix well.

Boil the liquid, reduce heat to medium low and simmer the stew, covered, for 1½ hours, stirring occasionally. Discard the ginger.

If you like, add a few drops of roasted sesame oil before serving. This casserole serves four people and needs no rice or noodles as the vegetables make it quite hearty. Takes one hour and 45 minutes.

Clams with Black Bean-Garlic Sauce   Serves 2

This recipe is both a Middle Burner and a Kidney tonic, particularly good for Deficient Kidney Yin. Lilah Kan does it with in-the-shell clams as a side dish, but I prefer it with dried or canned clams, served with rice or Chinese noodles.

1-2 cans CLAMS (or 2-3 dozen DRIED CLAMS)

SESAME OIL (for frying black beans, garlic and onion)

1 MEDIUM ONION

1½ T. SALTED BLACK BEANS (rinsed, drained and mashed)

1 T. MINCED GARLIC

Braising Liquid

1 tsp. SOY SAUCE or TAMARI

¼ tsp. GINGER ROOT (finely grated)

¼ cup WATER

Put clams and braising liquid ingredients into a large heavy casserole.

Cook the onion, garlic, and black beans in a wok coated with cooking oil, stirring constantly for 3 minutes.

Transfer this mixture to the large casserole and bring it to a boil. Reduce heat to medium low and simmer the whole thing for 15 to 20 minutes.

Add a binder of 2 tsp. cornstarch mixed into 2 tsp. water; add a few drops of roasted sesame oil. Serve hot as a side dish or part of a larger Chinese meal.

Serves two as a main course, five to six as part of a larger meal. Takes 30 minutes to prepare.

Five Jewel Casserole   Serves 2

This recipe is a good Kidney tonic for a Deficient situation, it is a Blood tonic and it is anti-hypertensive. It can be adapted to the time of year in terms of ingredients.

15 to 25 DRIED OYSTERS

½ lb. FIRM TOFU or TEMPEH, cubed and slow fried on all sides

½ lb. CHINESE or ITALIAN SWEET SAUSAGE, cut into small pieces

1 can WATER CHESTNUTS, sliced

½ lb. SNOW PEAS or FROZEN PEAS

Braising Liquid

2 T. SOY SAUCE or TAMARI

2 T. COOKING SHERRY

½ tsp. HONEY or SUGAR

1 T. OYSTER SAUCE

½ cup OYSTER SOAKING LIQUID (reserved)

Soak the oysters in water for 24 hours, changing water twice. Drain and reserve the liquid from the last soak. Put oysters into a large casserole. Combine braising liquid and pour over the oysters. Bring to a boil, lower heat, and simmer for 30 minutes.

Add the pre-fried tofu or tempeh cubes and simmer another 15 minutes.

Pre-fry the sausage and add it, along with the peas and water chestnuts, to the casserole and simmer another 5 to 7 minutes.

Stir in a binder of 1 T. cornstarch mixed into 1 T. water with a few drops of sesame oil. Let the whole thing thicken a bit and serve hot with rice.

Takes about one hour to prepare plus the oyster soaking time and serves two as a main course, four to six as a side dish in a larger meal.

Eight Jade Casserole   Serves 3

Kidney and Lower Burner tonification is the main thrust of this recipe, but you could alter the overall effect by adding other ingredients. Chicken is warming to the entire body and specially to the Middle Burner/Stomach fire. A wonderful winter meal with rice or noodles, it is also a tonic for Kidney Yin Deficiency.

6-8 DRIED BLACK MUSHROOMS

LETTUCE LEAVES (for lining the casserole)

8-12 SHRIMP, dried or fresh (if fresh, peel and de-vein)

4 CHICKEN LIVERS, trimmed and halved

8 CHICKEN HEARTS

4 CHICKEN GIZZARDS, halved

3 or 4 SMALL SQUID, fresh or dried (cut in 1-inch pieces)

SESAME OIL

¼ to ½ lb. CHINESE or ITALIAN SWEET SAUSAGE or BAR-BECUED PORK

1 cup PEAS or SNOW PEAS, frozen or fresh

Marinade

2 T. SOY SAUCE or TAMARI

2 T. COOKING SHERRY

½ tsp. HONEY or SUGAR

2 CLOVES MINCED GARLIC

¼ tsp. FRESH GINGER ROOT, grated

¼ tsp. ROASTED SESAME OIL

Braising Liquid

½ cup MUSHROOM-SOAKING LIQUID

½ cup CHICKEN BROTH

3 T. OYSTER SAUCE

¼ tsp. WHITE PEPPER

Soak mushrooms in water for one hour. Drain them, reserving the liquid. Remove and discard the stems and chop into quarters.

Line a large heavy casserole with fresh lettuce leaves.

Mix the marinade ingredients, stirring until the sweetener dissolves. Put the shrimp, livers, gizzards, hearts, and squid in one bowl, cover with marinade and leave at room temperature for one hour. (Note: if using dried squid, it must soak overnight or at least 8 hours for the best results.)

In a hot wok coated with cooking oil fry the chopped sausage. When it is about half done, add the marinated ingredients and stir-fry over medium heat until the livers and gizzards are brown in color.

Transfer the stir-fried ingredients to the casserole; add the mushrooms and peas.

Combine the braising liquid ingredients and pour into the casserole. Bring to a boil, reduce heat to medium low and simmer for 30 minutes.

Stir two teaspoons cornstarch into two teaspoons cold water, mix into the liquid, add a few drops roasted sesame oil, let the whole thing thicken a bit, and serve hot with noodles or rice.

It takes about one hour to soak and marinate the ingredients, one half hour to prepare and 30 minutes to cook. Serves three as a main dish.

Chinese Paella Serves 6 to 8

This would be contraindicated in any Hot or Damp/Wet conditions as it is very lubricating. It is nourishing to the Kidneys, has an overall warming effect on the body, and is an excellent Lubricant for Dry Lung.

1 WHOLE CHICKEN BREAST, boned and cut into 1-inch chunks

½ lb or more FRESH SHRIMP, peeled and de-veined, or ¼ to ½ lb. DRIED SHRIMP, soaked for 6 to 8 hours

3 cups LONG GRAIN BROWN RICE (or WHITE RICE, which is easier to digest but has fewer nutrients)

1 lb. CHINESE or ITALIAN SWEET SAUSAGE

12 DRIED MUSSELS OR OYSTERS (soaked overnight, cut in half)

1½ cups FROZEN PEAS, thawed

Marinade

2 T. SOY SAUCE or TAMARI

2 T. COOKING SHERRY

½ tsp. HONEY or SUGAR

2 CLOVES GARLIC, finely minced

¼ tsp. GINGER ROOT, fresh grated

½ tsp. ROASTED SESAME OIL

Pre-soak oysters or mussels for 24 hours, drain and chop in half.

Stir marinade ingredients together, dissolving sweetener. Put the chicken and shrimp into two separate bowls and pour half the marinade over each. Marinate for one hour at room temperature.

Meanwhile, wash the rice *thoroughly*, removing all starch. Use a large 4-quart casserole, add rice, and cover with an inch of water.

Cover the rice and bring to a boil. Add chicken, shrimp, sausage, mussels, or oysters and cook over a low heat for 15 minutes if white rice is used, or 35 minutes if brown rice is used. Sprinkle in the peas and cook for 15 more minutes. Give it all a stir, or add a few drops of sesame oil if you wish and serve hot with a nice white wine.

Chinese Remedial Recipes

In Chengdu, the capitol of Sichuan (Szechuan), there is a restaurant next to a Chinese pharmacy. As in some Chinese pharmacies, there is an herbal doctor who works in the store diagnosing and writing prescriptions for patients. These prescriptions also include specific meals at the restaurant next door. This restaurant specializes in preparing dishes which embody the therapeutic principles of classical Chinese medicine. Many of the dishes served there use exotic medicinal ingredients such as cobra and scaly anteater and there is little distinction between herbs and vegetables. Unfortunately there is not a health food restaurant in America that can compare with this kind of therapeutic specificity.

Below are a number of recipes which are both delicious, easy to prepare, and specifically indicated for treatment of Chinese energetic syndromes and the symptoms engendered by such imbalances. After becoming familiar with the energetic natures of individual foods, both practitioner and patient should attempt to analyze the rationale for each food in a recipe. This is similar to rationalizing the construction of an acupuncture formula or an herbal prescription. Once you are proficient in this, go to a Chinese restaurant and try to figure out what syndrome(s) each dish on the menu would be therapeutic for as well as its contraindications. This can be a fun and quick way to begin thinking in terms of Chinese dietary therapy.

Chinese Peanut Butter
Sesame Seed Cookies   Serves 10

This delightful dessert is as well an excellent Stomach/Spleen Deficiency treatment. It will also aid in soothing a Dry Lung condition.

Filling

2 T. WHOLE WHEAT FLOUR or UNBLEACHED FLOUR

½ cup TOASTED SESAME SEEDS

1¼ T. PEANUT BUTTER (or a bit more)

4 T. RAISINS

WATER (enough to make a thick paste)

Pastry

2 cups FLOUR

½ cup BROWN SUGAR

2 T. BUTTER or LARD

4 T. WATER

1 EGG YOLK

Parch the flour in a dry pan until it is light brown. Grind the sesame seeds to a paste in a mortar and pestle or blender. Add these to the other ingredients and stir to make a thick paste. Divide into ten portions and set aside.

Mix the pastry flour and sugar together and divide into two uneven portions, about 40% and 60%. Mix the smaller portion with the butter and knead to make a dough. Roll each portion separately. Place one layer on top of the other and fold into four or six layers. Roll the layered dough again. Repeat the folding and rolling process three or four times. Then cut the dough into 20 pieces and roll these into 20 circles.

Place a portion of the filling on each of the ten circles. Put the other ten circles on top to form a sandwich. Fold the edges inward diagonally to form a small, attractive pie. Brush the top of each with beaten egg yolk. Bake at 350° for 20 minutes or until light brown.

Spinach with Creamed Crab Sauce   Serves 4

This is a very nourishing recipe, which is created to lower Hyper Liver Yang, cool Liver Fire, and bring the energy in the body down. If mustard greens are substituted for the spinach, it is a very useful recipe for the treatment of Damp Sputum Cough or Congested Lungs.

4 oz. CRAB MEAT
14 oz. FRESH WASHED SPINACH, stems removed
4 T. PEANUT or SESAME OIL
5 oz. MILK or CREAM
½ tsp. SALT
1 tsp. CORNSTARCH
1 T. WATER
SALT TO TASTE

Clean the crab meat, chop up, and place in a saucepan with the milk or cream and set aside.

Chop the spinach and heat the oil and salt in a pan. Saute spinach on high heat for a few minutes, then remove from pan and drain.

Now cook the crab/milk mixture for a few minutes. Add the cornstarch/water binder and stir until thickened. Taste to see if the mixture needs salt.

Spread the spinach on a platter, pour the crab sauce over it and serve hot.

Takes about 15 to 20 minutes to prepare. Serves four as a side dish.

Chinese Tomato Soup   Serves 4

This recipe is surprising in that the Chinese use very few tomatoes in their cooking. This recipe is specifically for lowering and cooling a Hyper Yang Liver.

2 LARGE FRESH TOMATOES (canned tomatoes are smaller: use 4)
1 ONION
3½ T. VEGETABLE OIL
2 T. CHOPPED BACON or ITALIAN SAUSAGE
4 cups HOT WATER
1 CHICKEN or BEEF BOUILLON CUBE
1½ tsp. salt
1 EGG

Remove stems from tomatoes and cut into six triangular wedges. Cut onion in the same way as tomatoes.

Heat oil in a wok or deep pan and saute the onion, tomatoes, and bacon for a few minutes. Add the hot water and bouillon cube and bring to a boil. Reduce heat and simmer for five minutes.

Season with salt. Stir in the beaten egg little by little quickly over a high heat and serve hot.

Takes about 15 to 20 minutes to prepare and serves four as a first course.

Kidney Abalone Saute   Serves 2

This recipe has many therapeutic uses. It calms nerves, functions as a Blood tonic and as a Kidney Yin Deficiency Tonic, and treats Kidney Yin Deficiency and Liver Deficiency. It is also very tasty.

1 PORK KIDNEY
5 oz. canned ABALONE
5 or 6 DRIED BLACK MUSHROOMS
2 T. SESAME or PEANUT OIL
PINCH OF SALT
¼ lb. SNOW PEAS, fresh or frozen
2½ tsp. CORNSTARCH
4 T. BROTH FROM CANNED ABALONE
1 tsp. SALT

Cut kidney in half and remove the white muscle. Score each side of the kidney and cut into large bite-sized pieces. Soak these pieces in water in a saucepan, then boil briefly.

Cut the abalone in the same sized pieces.

Soak the mushrooms in water until soft (about one hour), then remove stems and cut into quarters.

Heat 1 T. of the oil in a wok and saute the mushrooms, seasoning with salt. Remove from pan and set aside.

Heat the remaining oil and saute the kidney for a few minutes. Add the mushrooms, abalone, and peas. Saute three to five minutes.

Make binder of cornstarch and abalone juice and pour it in, stirring until thick. Serve hot.

Takes about 30 to 40 minutes to prepare. Serves two as a single dish with rice, or four as part of a larger meal.

Mushu Chicken (Chinese Pancakes)   Serves 4

This dish is a nice Stomach/Spleen tonic, while at the same time is cooling to a Hyper Yang Liver.

Dough

1¾ cups WHOLE WHEAT FLOUR or UNBLEACHED WHITE FLOUR

½ cup WATER

1 T. SESAME OIL

OIL FOR FRYING

Filling

½ lb. BONELESS CHICKEN

½ tsp. COOKING SHERRY

PINCH OF SALT

1 LEEK, chopped into ¼-inch sections

2 DRIED CHINESE MUSHROOMS
or 1½ oz. sliced BUTTON MUSHROOMS)

½ GREEN PEPPER, washed and chopped into ½-inch squares

3 T. SESAME or PEANUT OIL

PINCH OF SALT

½ tsp. SOY SAUCE or TAMARI

½ cup PINENUTS

Bean Paste

3 T. SESAME OIL mixed with:

3 oz. MISO PASTE,

3 T. SUGAR,

3 T. WATER, or a little more.

Mix flour with water and knead into a soft dough. Form into a long sausage shape and cut into 20 pieces. Flatten each piece into a round disc. Brush 10 of the discs with the sesame seed oil. Place the 10 ungreased pieces of dough on top of the oiled ones.

Roll out these "sandwiches" to seven inches or so in diameter. Lightly grease a pan and fry each one over low heat on both sides. They will separate during frying. Set all 20 pieces aside on a serving plate.

Chop the chicken, season with sherry and salt. Wash and chop the leek. Soak the mushrooms in hot water for 30 to 60 minutes. Drain and dice, discarding the stems. Chop green peppers.

Heat oil in a wok and saute chicken first, then add the leek, the mushrooms and finally the green pepper. Add a pinch of salt and soy sauce and pine nuts. Saute briefly and remove from wok to serving dish.

Mix bean paste ingredients.

Serve all three dishes and at the table place one tablespoon of the filling on each pancake and roll up. The bean paste is the condiment.

This takes one hour to prepare and serves four or five as the main dish.

Hwang Qi
with Chicken Essence Soup   Serves 3 to 4

This recipe is also an "herbal" treatment, as it includes hwang chi (astragalus) as one of the ingredients. It is used to strengthen the Stomach/Spleen, reduce hypertension, and as an aid in treatment of diabetes.

1 CHICKEN for boiling
2 grams ASTRAGALUS (Hwang Qi)
1 tsp. GINGER JUICE
½ tsp. SALT (or more to taste)
1 to 2 tsp. COOKING SHERRY, MIRIN, or SAKE

Stew the chicken in a pot with 4 cups of water for about one hour. At the same time, cook the hwang chi in two cups of water until it boils down to one cup. Then add the hwang chi and other ingredients to the larger pot and stew until the smell of the alcohol disappears. Strain the soup and serve only the broth. Serves three to four as an appetizer.

Quick Preserved Vegetable Saute   Serves 2

This dish promotes a stronger appetite, reduces Hyper Liver Yang, and strengthens the nerves.

½ lb. SLIVERED PORK MEAT
1 CHOPPED LEEK
1 small can CHINESE PRESERVED VEGETABLE
8 PIECES LONG BEAN or ½ lb. FRESH GREEN BEANS
1 CRUSHED CLOVE GARLIC
1 SLIVER OF GINGER, minced
¼ to ½ lb. CHOPPED BROCCOLI
¼ lb. FINELY CHOPPED BAMBOO SHOOTS

If using long bean, soak in boiling water half an hour, then peel. Otherwise, clean the usual way and parboil for five minutes and drain.

Heat 3 to 4 tablespoons of oil in a wok and saute the pork, leek, ginger, garlic, and broccoli until the pork turns brown. Add the bamboo shoots and vegetables; saute for five more minutes. Turn off the stove and add the beans, with enough soy sauce to season. Serve hot with rice, noodles or another grain.

Abalone Chicken Paste Soup   Serves 4 to 6

This recipe is specifically for persons suffering from a Hyper Yang Liver who also have a marked Yin Deficiency. It is very easy to prepare and is a nice appetizer.

2 PIECES OF ABALONE	
¼ cup CHOPPED CHICKEN MEAT	
¼ cup SLIVERED, PRECOOKED HAM	
½ tsp. SALT	
5 to 6 cups WATER	

Clean and sliver the abalone. Soak the raw chicken in hot water for half an hour and sliver it as well.

Place all ingredients over a medium flame and boil for 15 minutes. Skim any bubbles and serve the soup hot. This takes 45 minutes to prepare.

Quick Braised Soybean Sprouts   Serves 1 to 2

This recipe relieves hypertension and is good for the nervous system. It also tends to be somewhat diuretic.

1 cup SOYBEAN SPROUTS	
3 tsp. SESAME OIL	
SALT, PEPPER, and SOY SAUCE or TAMARI to taste	

Wash the sprouts and remove roots if there are any.

Heat a wok over a high flame and pour in sesame oil. When oil is hot braise the sprouts for 30 seconds. Remove from heat and stir in the other ingredients to taste. Serve immediately.

This takes ten minutes to prepare and serves one to two as a side dish.

Assorted Cucumber and Mung Bean
Thread Noodles   Serves 2

This dish is surprisingly tasty and has several therapeutic uses. It lowers Hyper Liver Yang, is strengthening to the nervous system, soothes nervousness, and improves the appetite.

2 CUCUMBERS OF MEDIUM SIZE
¼ lb. BEAN THREAD NOODLES
1 to 2 T. SLIVERED PRECOOKED HAM or CHINESE HAM
½ tsp. SALT
1½ tsp. APPLE CIDER or RED WINE VINEGAR
1 T. SESAME OIL
½ tsp. HONEY or SUGAR
½ tsp. PREPARED MUSTARD
1 T. TOASTED SESAME SEEDS

Toast sesame seeds in a dry pan and set aside. Boil four cups of water and soak the noodles in this water (turn off flame), for three to five minutes, until soft.

Saute the cucumber and ham in the sesame oil over high heat for one minute. Quickly add all the other ingredients to the sauteed cucumbers and stir again.

Quickly mix the noodles and the sauteed ingredients and serve hot.

This takes half an hour or less to prepare and serves two people with one other dish.

Nori Egg Drop Soup

Serves 4 to 6

This recipe is particularly good for anyone with hypertension if the physician fears that the patient will or could have a stroke. It sedates Hyper Liver Yang. This is a general Yin Tonic and is good for Lung Tonification as long as the Lungs are not in a cold condition.

2 SHEETS OF NORI
3 EGGS
6 cups PREPARED CHICKEN BROTH
¼ cup MINCED LEEK or SCALLION
¼ tsp. MINCED FRESH GINGER
1 T. COOKING SHERRY
DASH OF ROASTED SESAME OIL

Toast the nori sheets quickly over a flame or burner until they change color from purple to green and then brush them and add to the chicken broth in a large pot. Simmer for ten minutes.

Gently pour in the slightly beaten eggs, add the other ingredients and give the mixture a stir. Serve as soon as the eggs appear cooked.

If you make the chicken broth yourself, this takes two hours or so to prepare. If you buy it canned or use bouillon cubes, it takes about 15 minutes. It serves four to six people as an appetizer.

In addition to aiding the cooling of a Hyper Yang Liver, this recipe also benefits the function of the Liver in general and the Heart as well. This recipe is excellent in transforming Sputum and clearing Heat in a Hot Lung condition.

1 oz. (5 or 6) DRIED MUSHROOMS	
1 ABALONE FILLET	
½ cup SNOW PEAS (fresh or frozen)	
½ tsp. SALT	
1 T. SESAME OIL	
1 tsp. SOY SAUCE or TAMARI	
½ tsp. HONEY or SUGAR	
1 T. MINCED LEEK or SCALLION	
1 SLICE FRESH GINGER	
2 CLOVES CRUSHED GARLIC	
1 tsp. CORNSTARCH, dissolved in 3 cups (or more) water	

Soak the mushrooms for one hour, then remove stems and sliver.

Sliver the abalone into small pieces.

Heat the oil in a wok, add the leek, garlic, ginger, and mushroom, and quickly braise for half a minute or a little more. Add the abalone and peas and stir for another half a minute. Then add the water and cornstarch mixture and stir until it thickens slightly.

This takes one hour soaking time and fifteen minutes to prepare. It serves four as an appetizer.

Oxtail Tomato Soup   Serves 6 to 8

This dish is not dissimilar to its Western counterpart. Its special function is to strengthen a Deficient Stomach/Spleen and improve a Deficient Blood condition.

½ lb. OXTAIL(S)
1 STICK CELERY
¾ lb. FRESH TOMATOES, chopped in 6 or 8 pieces
4 CLOVES GARLIC, minced or crushed
1 MEDIUM ONION, chopped in large chunks
¼ tsp. each CRUSHED ANISEED AND CLOVES
tsp. BLACK PEPPER
1 T. COOKING SHERRY

Chop the oxtail into small pieces and rinse in boiling water.

Chop the onion, tomato, and celery. Mince the garlic.

Put 4 T. of oil in a hot wok and fry the oxtail. Add 10 cups of water to the wok after about six or seven minutes of frying and skim off any bubbles that are on the surface. Add the anise seeds and cloves and cover the mixture, allowing it to simmer for 30 minutes.

In another pan, fry the onion, celery, garlic, and tomato for several minutes until the onion is transparent. Then add this to the larger wok or pot with the oxtail in it.

Add all the remaining ingredients and simmer until half the water is gone.

This takes an hour and a half to prepare and serves six to eight.

Chicken and Walnut Saute   Serves 2

This is an excellent recipe for the treatment of Blood Deficiency Insomnia or postpartum insomnia and the related neuroses or nervous conditions. It is an excellent Kidney Yin Deficiency tonic and will also warm the Lungs if they are in a Cold/Dry condition.

10 WALNUTS, halved or quartered
½ to ¾ lb. CHOPPED CHICKEN MEAT, precooked
5 SMALL PIECES BLACK FUNGUS (Chinese dried), soaked and slivered
1 SMALL GREEN CHILI PEPPER, minced
1 EGG WHITE
4 CHINESE DRIED MUSHROOMS, soaked, stemmed, and slivered
1 tsp. MINCED SCALLION
½ tsp. MINCED FRESH GINGER
1 CLOVE CRUSHED GARLIC
1 T. COOKING SHERRY
1 tsp. SOY SAUCE or TAMARI
½ tsp. SALT
½ tsp. HONEY or SUGAR
½ cup TOASTED SESAME SEEDS

Soak the walnuts in hot water until the skins loosen. Peel them and fry in oil with the chicken, one scrambled egg white, and the other ingredients. Saute for five to seven minutes and serve hot.

This takes thirty to forty minutes to prepare and serves two with rice.

Sweet Potato Porridge   Serves 2

This dish is very nourishing and improves a Deficient Stomach/Spleen condition as well as benefiting a Deficient Kidney situation. It would be an excellent dish for anyone recuperating from a long illness or in a weak postpartum situation. It is a Deficiency Tonic for both Lungs and Kidneys.

½ lb. YAM or SWEET POTATO, sliced thin

1 cup WHITE RICE

¼ cup LOTUS SEEDS

1 CARROT, cut in very thin half moons

¼ cup JOB'S TEARS (Chinese barley)

3 or 4 CHOPPED LONGANS (dried)

½ tsp. SALT (or more to taste)

Few dashes ROASTED SESAME OIL

Cut carrot and yam as directed and simmer all ingredients except the salt and sesame oil with five cups water for seven to eight hours or overnight.

Stir in salt and sesame oil and serve warm, with a little honey if desired.

This takes eight hours (or overnight) to prepare and serves two large or four small portions.

Mutton (Lamb) Soup with Tang-kuei   Serves 1

This recipe is a wonderful Blood tonic for anyone who has anemia, irregular menstruation, or other Blood Deficiency/Stagnation symptoms. It is excellent for Yin Deficient Kidneys.

½ lb. SLIVERED LAMB MEAT
2 CHOPPED WALNUTS
5 RED CHINESE DATES
10 grams TANG-KUEI
10 grams DRIED LONGAN, slivered
1 STAR ANISE SEED
1/8 tsp. BLACK PEPPER
1 tsp. MINCED SCALLION
1 THIN SLICE of FRESH GINGER
1 T. RICE WINE or COOKING SHERRY
½ tsp. SALT (or more to taste)
1 tsp. SOY SAUCE or TAMARI

Boil the mutton in 2 cups water with the scallions and ginger for ten minutes. Skim off any bubbles on the surface.

Add the other ingredients except the soy sauce and wine and cook for ten more minutes. Remove the tang-kuei root (unless powder is used) and the slice of ginger.

Add soy sauce and wine and serve hot. (This can also simmer over a low flame for a long time if desired.)

This takes thirty minutes to prepare and serves one.

Sesame Dumplings   Serves 3 to 5

This is really a therapeutic dessert. It will improve a situation of Dry Blood or Fluid Deficiency Constipation.

½ cup SWEET RICE FLOUR
1 T. BLACK SESAME SEEDS
3 CHOPPED OR CRUSHED WALNUTS
1½ tsp. PINENUTS, chopped in half
2 T. SESAME OIL or VEGETABLE OIL
2 T. STRAWBERRY JAM or BLACKBERRY JAM
1 T. HONEY or SUGAR

Simmer the walnut, pinenut, sesame seed, sugar, and jam for 15 to 20 minutes in a small sauce pan.

Add water a little at a time to the sweet rice flour until you can knead into a soft but workable dough. Divide into balls. Flatten each ball (you should have 12 to 18, depending upon how big you make them) and put a teaspoon or so of the filling into it and fold together to make a stuffed ball.

After all are filled, boil six or more cups of water and drop several dumplings into the water. When the dumplings rise to the surface they are done. Water must be kept boiling. Repeat this process until all are done. Keep the finished ones in a warm oven until ready to serve. Makes a wonderful breakfast for three to five people with tea.

Eight Treasure Rice Pudding   Serves 4 to 6

This is a very popular dessert in China called Pa-Pao (Eight Treasure Rice). It is almost like a rice fruitcake and is eaten as a breakfast or a dessert. It is a wonderful Blood Deficiency Tonic as well as being good for Stomach/Spleen Deficiency.

3 cups SWEET RICE, washed
¾ cup CHESTNUT FLOUR (or chickpea flour or sweet rice flour)
½ cup PINENUTS, cut in half
½ cup RAISINS
1 T. LOTUS SEEDS
3 DRIED PRUNES, chopped
3 DRIED LYCHEE NUTS, pitted and chopped
4 or 5 DATES (red or brown), chopped
2 or 3 pieces CHOPPED DRIED PINEAPPLE and ORANGE PEEL (glazed type)
½ cup SUGAR
1 T. CORNSTARCH
1 T. BUTTER or VEGETABLE OIL

Cook rice with 3¾ cups water until done (40 to 50 minutes). Add butter or oil and sugar.

Place the dates and raisins around the bottom of a well-greased bowl which will fit into a steamer of bamboo or onto the steamer tray of your wok. Mix the nuts, prunes, lychee, and dried fruits into the rice. Then put this mixture gently into the bowl so as not to disturb your fruit arrangement.

Mix the chestnut or sweet rice flour into a paste with a little water and honey or sugar and spread it into the bowl over the rice. Steam this in a bamboo steamer or in a wok with a steamer tray for 15 to 20 minutes. Overturn the bowl onto a plate and then make a syrup out of cornstarch, butter and honey and drizzle over the top. Serve warm.

This can also be made in smaller bowls for individual desserts or breakfasts. It takes about an hour and a half to prepare and serves four or six as a dessert.

Mushroom Winter Melon Soup　　　　　　Serves 2

A dual purpose is served with this dish because it is a tonic for a Deficient Kidney and Heart as well as to lower a Hyper Yang Liver. It can be used for both Yin Deficient Lungs and Kidneys and also to help eliminate Sputum.

1 lb. WINTER MELON, cubed into 1-inch pieces
¼ oz. HWANG QI (astragalus), washed and chopped, soaked for 2 hours
3 to 4 DRIED BLACK MUSHROOMS, soaked for one hour, stemmed, and chopped
4 oz. DRIED WAKAME (or alaria seaweed), soaked for one hour and drained
½ tsp. GINGER JUICE
½ tsp. SALT (or more to taste)
1 T. RICE WINE or COOKING SHERRY
1 tsp. SOY SAUCE or TAMARI
2 T. DRIED SHRIMP, soaked for one hour or more

Wash and chop the hwang chi, mushroom, and seaweed and cut into fine slivers. Place these in 2 ½ to 3 cups of water and boil, then simmer.

Add the winter melon cubes and the rest of the ingredients. Cook for half and hour and serve hot.

This takes two hours of soaking time and 45 to 50 minutes to cook. It serves two or three (or one person for more than one meal!)

Dragon Eye Pudding   Serves 4

This is a wonderful Blood tonic for Deficiency/Stagnation problems such as postpartum anemia. It is also wonderfully simple to make.

1 13-oz. can LONGANS (sweetened)

3 T. RICE FLOUR

1 tsp. BRANDY (flavored brandy or triple sec)

Drain longans and reserve enough syrup to make two cups with added liquor and water if needed (add liquor first).

Combine liquid with rice flour in a saucepan and bring to a slow boil, stirring constantly, and cook until it thickens (about 10 to 12 minutes).

Add longans and serve hot or warm in individual bowls. You may also substitute lichee fruits if you like.

This takes 15 minutes to make and serves four.

Sweet Rice Congee
with Shrimp and Walnuts   Serves 2

This recipe is listed separately because sweet rice is not diuretic as is regular rice, and so may be eaten safely by people with a tendency to polyuria or nocturia. Also the walnuts tonify the nerves, and the shrimp tones and benefits the Qi and Blood.

1 cup SWEET RICE

4 cups WATER

15 DRIED SHRIMP, soaked and drained

7 to 10 WALNUTS, crushed

Place all ingredients into a large pot, put heat on simmer and leave eight hours or overnight. Stir in the morning and serve hot or warm with a little honey and/or salt.

Shrimp, Chicken, Water Chestnut and Mushroom Rice Pot

Serves 2

This easy dish is an excellent treatment for a Damp Spleen and a hearty appetite.

---

15 FRESH OR DRIED SHRIMP (if dried, soak and drain)

½ to 1 lb. CHICKEN, partially pre-cooked and chopped into bite-sized chunks

---

6 to 8 DRIED BLACK MUSHROOMS, soaked, drained, stemmed

---

12 DRIED CHESTNUTS, soaked overnight or longer

1½ cups WHITE RICE

SALT and SOY SAUCE TO TASTE

WATER (as needed)

Wash the rice thoroughly, rinsing several times until rinse water is clear. Place in a large Dutch oven or lidded baking casserole. Add water until it is just shy of the top of your thumb knuckle.

Add all other ingredients except salt and soy sauce. Stir and cover. Place in a 375° oven for 30 minutes, and don't lift the lid until then. Then uncover, add salt and soy sauce to taste, cooking sherry if you like, or a dash of roasted sesame oil. Give it a stir and serve hot.

If the rice is not cooked enough after 30 minutes, replace the lid and cook for an additional ten. This takes 45 minutes and serves two to three large appetites.

American Remedial Recipes

The recipes in this section are all based on American cuisine. They are not specifically Oriental. However they are remedial in the treatment of illnesses and imbalances as categorized by classical Chinese medicine. Whether a food is Chinese or American is beside the point. French, Italian, and Mexican cuisines are hardly regarded as foreign in the States and American cuisine is by its very nature multi-cultural. No matter what the country of origin, the important thing is the therapeutic principles a dish embodies. A recipe could be from Timbuktu and still be perfectly valid in the treatment of a disease according to Chinese medicine. I am stressing this point because I believe it is necessary to eliminate as much as possible any reverse cultural chauvinism. Chinese dietary therapy and Chinese-style medicine are valuable not because they are exotic and Oriental but because they are based on cosmic principles which are more profound and ultimately more practical than those upon which most other forms of healing are currently based.

This most nourishing of pies is excellent for Deficient Stomach/Spleen. It is also excellent for Blood Deficiency and Stagnation, and is a tonic for Deficient Kidneys and Lungs.

---

1 RECIPE OF YOUR FAVORITE PIE CRUST (use WHOLE WHEAT pastry flour)

1¾ to 2 cups COOKED, MASHED YAMS

---

3 BEATEN EGGS, room temperature

½ to ¾ cup BROWN SUGAR, BARLEY MALT, SYRUP, OR HONEY

---

1 tsp. CINNAMON

½ tsp. CLOVES

¼ tsp. NUTMEG

½ tsp. ALLSPICE

---

1 scant tsp. SALT

1½ cups EVAPORATED MILK (or mixed NONFAT DRY MILK, GOAT MILK, SOY MILK or CASHEW MILK)

WHIPPED CREAM for the top (optional)

Prepare crust and put into a 9 to 10 inch pie plate.

In a large bowl, beat together all the other ingredients except whipped cream. Beat thoroughly, preferably with an electric mixer or blender. Pour this into the pie shell and bake in a preheated 375° oven for almost an hour. Cool before serving.

This pie takes one hour to prepare and another to bake, and serves six to eight people.

Amasake Cheesecake with Cherry Topping

Serves 6 to 8

The fermented sweet rice filling is an excellent tonic for Deficient Spleen, while the cherries tone the Qi and Blood and help remove any rheumatic pain in the body. Also a possible treatment for Blood Deficiency and Stagnation.

2 cups	PREPARED AMASAKE
1½ cups	WATER
2½ tsp.	AGAR FLAKES
1 tsp.	UMEBOSHI PASTE (or use 2 tsp. CIDER VINEGAR and ½ tsp. SALT)
1 T.	HONEY or BARLEY MALT
3 tsp.	VANILLA EXTRACT
1 T.	LEMON JUICE

Make your favorite pastry or graham cracker crust and pre-bake for 20 minutes at 350°, covered with baking paper and pie weights or beans.

Mix all ingredients in a blender and pour into the pre-baked shell, baking the whole thing another 20 minutes at the same temperature. Let all this cool for one hour and then top with:

1 cup	CHERRIES
½ cup	APPLE JUICE
¼ cup	HONEY
¼ tsp.	SALT
1 tsp.	CORNSTARCH, ARROWROOT, or KUDZU ROOT

Cook these ingredients all together in a small saucepan and when thickened, put on top of the cake. Cool to room temperature.

Note: ready-made amasake is usually available in natural food store delicatessens. If not, you can get a recipe for it when you buy Cold Mountain Brand Koji. It can be made with regular or sweet rice, although sweet rice is preferable.

This takes 1¼ hours to prepare if using prepared amasake. It serves six to eight people.

Shepherd's Pie
with Beef or Chicken   Serves 5 or 6

This is one of our favorite winter meals and is always a winner with guests. It will strengthen a Deficient Spleen and warm the entire body. This recipe is a Kidney Yin Tonic.

1 LARGE or 2 MEDIUM CARROTS
2 MEDIUM POTATOES
2 MEDIUM ONIONS
1 SMALL HEAD CABBAGE
ANY OTHER VEGETABLES (*except* bell peppers or tomatoes)
2 T. SESAME OIL or SOY OIL
2 to 3 LARGE CLOVES GARLIC, minced or crushed
1 T. CRUSHED, DRIED BASIL
1½ tsp. RUBBED THYME
1 tsp. SALT
¼ tsp. BLACK PEPPER
1 cup COOKING SHERRY or RICE WINE (sherry is best here)
2 T. CORNSTARCH or ARROWROOT, dissolved in ¼ cup water
1 lb. CUBED BEEF (chuck or rump roast is fine) OR: 1 lb. BONED, SLIVERED CHICKEN MEAT

Chop onion into thin moons, mince or crush the garlic and saute together in a large cast iron pan or Dutch oven. If using chicken you may saute this as well. Set aside.

120

In a large soup pot, put all the other vegetables. You will need to adjust the sizes so that the carrots will not still be hard while the potatoes get mushy, but the chunks should be fairly large. Also, add the beef and spices, the oil left over from sauteing the onion, and the sherry. Bring all this to a boil, lower heat to medium low and let simmer until the carrots are just tender, *not* soft or mushy. Strain off the liquid and set it aside. Put the vegetables into the large Dutch oven or cast iron casserole pot, with the onions and garlic.

Add about 1½ cups of this liquid to the already dissolved cornstarch. If you like, add another dollop of cooking sherry, too. Mix in the salt and pepper and pour this over the vegetables and meat. Place this, with a lid, into a 350° oven for 20 minutes while you prepare the following biscuit:

Biscuit   Serves 5 to 6

2 cups	WHOLE WHEAT PASTRY FLOUR
2 tsp.	NON-ALUMINUM BAKING POWDER
5 to 6 T.	BUTTER or QUALITY MARGARINE
½ tsp.	SALT
¼ tsp.	BAKING SODA
to ¾ cup	BUTTERMILK, SOUR MILK or YOGURT (raw milk or yogurt is best)

Cut the margarine or butter into the dry ingredients which have already been mixed together in a large bowl. Then add yogurt or milk and mix quickly just until all the flour is sticky and comes away from the sides of the bowl.

Remove the casserole from the oven and uncover. Place the biscuit evenly over the casserole, turn up heat to 400° and bake for 20 to 25 minutes until the biscuit is browned and an inserted toothpick shows no dough. If you prefer more of a "dumpling" effect, you can put the lid on while the biscuit cooks, but take it off for the last five minutes only.

Let the pie cool for 15 to 20 minutes before serving. This takes two or two and a half hours to prepare and bake and serves five or six people with a salad or other side dish.

Shepherd's Pie
with Seitan (Gluten Meat)   Serves 2

If Seitan is substituted in the above recipe for the beef or chicken, the dish becomes a good Yin tonic as well as a Spleen tonic and a therapeutic dish for a Hyper Yang Liver as well. Gluten is often available in bulk at natural food stores or canned in Chinese food markets. Preparation is otherwise exactly the same.

Ginger Beef
or Ginger Seitan "Beef"   Serves 2 to 4

Both these dishes are Stomach/Spleen tonics, but with the seitan the dish is also a treatment for a Hyper Yang Liver. The seitan is an excellent substitute for meat in cases where meat is restricted.

2 lbs. BEEF or SEITAN, presauteed and slivered
¼ cup FLOUR
1 tsp. SALT
½ tsp. BLACK PEPPER
2 tsp. FRESH GRATED or MINCED GINGER
1 tsp. TUMERIC
2 cups ONIONS, chopped fine
2 CLOVES CRUSHED or MINCED GARLIC
1 cup PLUM TOMATOES
1 or 2 dashes TABASCO
OIL for frying

Toss the beef slivers in a mixture of flour, salt, and powdered spices. Slowly fry this with ginger until browned on all sides and remove.

Saute onions and garlic, then return the meat or seitan to the pan with the other ingredients. Mix thoroughly. Cover and place in oven on low heat of 300° for one hour. If using seitan, be sure to check after 30 minutes that there is enough moisture. If not, add a little water.

Baked Mashed Turnips
or Daikon Radish

Serves 4

This recipe is incredibly easy and benefits a Damp Spleen. This is a perfect recipe for Damp Bi conditions.

2 to 3 lbs. TURNIPS or DAIKON RADISH, chopped

BUTTER, SALT, and PEPPER TO TASTE

Boil or pressure cook turnip or radish until soft. Drain and mash or blend until fairly smooth. Mix in butter, salt, and pepper to taste. Serve hot.

Sauteed (Stir-Fried) Daikon
with Scallion and Carrot

Serves 2

This dish could have been listed with American or with Chinese recipes since turnips can be substituted for daikon and sauteing is equally as good as frying in a wok. In any case, this recipe benefits a Deficient and Damp Spleen. This is great for all Damp Bi conditions.

1 LARGE DAIKON RADISH or 2 to 3 MEDIUM TURNIPS, cleaned and cut into half-moons

4 or more MEDIUM CARROTS, sliced diagonally into thin ovals

2 to 3 SCALLIONS, minced

SESAME OIL for frying

¼ tsp. SALT

SOY SAUCE TO TASTE

Heat a wok on high heat or a large skillet and add 1 to 2 T. oil. When it is hot add the carrots and daikon and stir-fry for two to three minutes. Then add scallions and stir-fry for another 30 to 60 seconds. Stir in salt, soy sauce, and a dash of black pepper if desired. Serve immediately.

Water Chestnut Soup   Serves 4

This soup is a very cooling, diuretic dish which should be used for the treatment of Hyper Liver Yang, or hypertension without the presence of polyuria.

---

6 to 8 WATER CHESTNUTS, sliced into one-eighth inch pieces

---

1 quart CHICKEN STOCK

---

8 oz. FRESH or FROZEN SPINACH, cleaned, chopped, and squeezed dry

---

SALT TO TASTE

Bring the chicken stock to a boil. If making your own stock, cook one chicken or several pieces of chicken in three quarts of water for one hour, strain, and set chicken aside for later use.

Lower heat on the pot of chicken stock and add salt and a dash or two of black pepper. Add chopped spinach and cook, stirring for two or three minutes. Pour into bowls and garnish with the sliced water chestnuts.

This soup takes fifteen to twenty minutes to prepare, unless you make your own chicken stock, in which case it takes 1½ hours. It serves four as a first course.

Gado Gado Sauce   Serves 4

This sauce is based on an Indonesian recipe and is often served with rice and whatever vegetables are in season. It is a Stomach/Spleen Deficiency dish which is quite warming to the Middle Burner.

---

1 to 1½ cups CHOPPED ONION

2 to 3 CLOVES CRUSHED GARLIC

1 cup plus 1 T. GOOD PEANUT BUTTER (unsalted)

1 T. HONEY or SUGAR

DASH CAYENNE POWDER

JUICE OF ONE LEMON

1½ tsp. GRATED FRESH GINGER ROOT

1 BAY LEAF, crushed

2½ cups WATER

1 T. CIDER VINEGAR

½ tsp. SALT

Dash TAMARI or SOY SAUCE

2 T. SESAME OIL or PEANUT OIL for frying

In a wok or large saucepan saute the onion, garlic, bay leaf, and ginger in oil until the onion is translucent. Then add remaining ingredients and mix thoroughly. Simmer on very low heat for 30 to 45 minutes, stirring occasionally.

Takes one hour to prepare and serves four people easily with rice, potatoes, fish or other vegetables.

Tuna Stuffed Peppers   Serves 4

This lovely dinner will help drain Excess Fluid and Cold Obstructions in the body. It would be excellent for anyone with rheumatism and is great for all Damp Bi conditions.

| 4 LARGE GREEN PEPPERS |
| BOILING WATER in a large pot |
| ¼ cup OLIVE OIL |
| ¼ cup MINCED SCALLION |
| 3 CLOVES CRUSHED GARLIC |
| 1½ cups WHOLE WHEAT or WHITE BREAD CRUMBS |
| 4 CHOPPED ANCHOVIES |
| 2 7-oz. can TUNA, drained and flaked |
| 1 LARGE TOMATO, peeled, cored, and finely chopped |
| 3 T. CAPERS (optional) |
| 3 T. MINCED FRESH PARSLEY |
| ½ tsp. OREGANO |
| ½ tsp. BASIL |
| JUICE OF ½ to 1 LEMON |
| 1 cup GRATED MOZZARELLA or PROVOLONE CHEESE |

Remove tops of peppers, remove cores and seeds and steam over boiling water for 10 minutes or a little more to soften, and set aside.

Preheat oven to 350-375°. Heat oil in a frying pan or wok and saute onion and garlic until onion is softened, three to five minutes. Add all other ingredients except lemon and cheese and stir well over heat for another two to three minutes.

Stuff the peppers and drizzle a bit of lemon juice over the top of each one. Bake them in a shallow baking dish with a little water in the bottom for 30 minutes. Sprinkle on cheese at that point and bake five more minutes until the cheese is melted and bubbling.

Takes about one hour to prepare and bake and serves four.

126

Lamb Kidneys Andalusian   Serves 2

This easy main dish is a tonic for both Yin and Yang Deficiency of the Kidneys. If lamb kidneys are unavailable, you may substitute one beef kidney instead. This is a close-to-perfect Yin Deficiency Tonic.

5 LAMB KIDNEYS
3 T. BUTTER
1 T. OLIVE OIL
1 tsp. MARJORAM
½ tsp. SALT
¼ tsp. BLACK PEPPER
10 BUTTON MUSHROOMS
1¼ cups MINCED ONION
½ cup COOKING SHERRY
¼ cup RED WINE or DRY WHITE WINE
½ tsp. SALT
¼ tsp. FRESHLY GROUND BLACK PEPPER
4 oz. COOKED NOODLES (4 oz. uncooked)

Remove fat and tubing on the underside of the kidneys with kitchen scissors. Cut crosswise into pieces about ¼-inch thick.

Melt the butter with oil in a large skillet and saute the kidneys, salt, pepper, and marjoram for two to three minutes until they have slightly browned and the juices have stopped running.

Remove kidneys from the pan and set aside. Add onion and mushrooms and saute three to four minutes until the sauce has begun to thicken. Reduce heat and add kidneys, cooking over low heat for two to three more minutes until kidneys are just heated through. Serve immediately over noodles.

This takes 30 minutes or less to prepare and serves two people.

Leek and Onion Pie   Serves 4

This wonderful entree helps remove Blood Stagnation and is tonifying to the Stomach and Spleen. It helps remove Stomach Heat, which can be the cause of fever blisters, mouth sores, halitosis, etc.

1 RECIPE OF YOUR FAVORITE PIE CRUST
4 LEEKS (3 if large), cleaned and chopped in ¼-inch slices
2 ONIONS, chopped into moon shapes
1 cup WATER
2 T. KUDZU ROOT POWDER or CORNSTARCH
1½ T. SOY SAUCE or TAMARI
Dash CIDER VINEGAR
Dash SALT and BLACK PEPPER

Line a pie dish with the crust. Do not flute edges. Preheat oven to 350°.

Saute the leeks and onion for 8-10 minutes in a wok or large skillet. Use butter or a high quality vegetable oil.

Dissolve the kudzu root or cornstarch in water with the soy sauce and add to the onion/leek mixture, stirring until it thickens. Add a dash of salt, pepper, and vinegar and pour into the waiting pie shell.

Roll out a top crust, lay it over the top, fluting edges nicely. Prick top to allow steam to escape and bake 35 to 45 minutes until crust is browned. Serve after 15 to 20 minutes of cooling time.

This takes just over one hour to prepare and serves four.

Seitan-Veal Marsala   Serves 3

Seitan is excellent for lowering Hyper Liver Yang and the Marsala sauce is a gentle Middle Burner tonic.

| ½ lb. PREPARED SEITAN (or wheat gluten "meat") |
| FLOUR for dredging cutlets |
| BUTTER for sauteing cutlets |
| 2 cups CLEANED, SLICED BUTTON MUSHROOMS |
| 2 tsp. CHOPPED SHALLOTS or SCALLIONS |
| 6 T. MARSALA WINE or COOKING SHERRY |
| ½ cup THIN MISO BROTH |

In a large, heavy-gauge fry pan, heat oil or butter while you dredge each cutlet in flour. Saute on all sides until browned. Remove from pan and set aside.

Put mushrooms and shallots or scallions into the pan drippings and stir constantly, until onions are soft and sauce begins to thicken, about five minutes. Return "veal" to pan and lower heat, cooking five more minutes. Serve hot over noodles or rice.

You'll find that this takes 45 minutes to prepare unless you make your own seitan. It serves three.

Corn Spoon Bread Pudding   Serves 6

Corn meal is a well known Heart tonic, and is also used in conditions of sexual weakness. Winter squash and honey tonify the Stomach/Spleen while apples lubricate the Upper Burner, making the overall recipe less warm in nature. A wonderful dessert for a cold winter night, not too sweet in nature. It can be made even a little warmer by using part oatmeal or oat flour.

3 cups	CORN MEAL
5 cups	WATER
2½ cups	CUBED BUTTERNUT SQUASH (or your favorite kind)
1½ tsp.	SALT
3	GRATED APPLES
3 T.	TAHINI or ALMOND BUTTER
½ cup	HONEY
½ cup	WHOLE WHEAT PASTRY FLOUR or UNBLEACHED FLOUR
2 T.	SOY FLOUR
1½ tsp.	CINNAMON
1 T.	GRATED ORANGE PEEL

Place corn meal, water, squash, and salt in a large saucepan or pot and bring to a boil. Lower heat and simmer for 20 minutes.

Puree this mixture in a blender until reasonably smooth. Stir in remaining ingredients. Taste and adjust salt, sweetener, and spices if you like.

Pour into an oiled or buttered two-quart casserole or large cake pan. Bake at 350° for 1½ hours. Serve hot or warm. People may want to melt a little bit of honey or butter on top. Wonderful.

Takes 45 minutes to prepare and one and a half hours to bake, serving six to eight people.

Delightful Date Bars

This recipe is quite warming and a good Stomach/Spleen tonic for a Deficiency condition. If you change the recipe to use apricots instead of dates, you also have a Heart tonic.

3 cups	PITTED DATES or DRIED APRICOTS
1 large T.	GRATED LEMON PEEL
¼ tsp.	SALT
2 cups	WATER
1 tsp.	VANILLA
1 cup	ROLLED OATS
½ cup	WHOLE WHEAT PASTRY FLOUR
½ cup	RICE FLOUR
1 cup	WHEAT GERM
¾ cup	UNSWEETENED SHREDDED COCONUT
¾ cup	MELTED BUTTER

Boil the dates or apricots, lemon peel, and salt in one cup of water. Mash the dates with a fork while they are cooking and when this is almost smooth add the vanilla and set aside.

Preheat oven to 350°. Mix dry ingredients in a bowl and then add the butter and mix in well. Heat one cup of water and pour over the dry mixture and stir in thoroughly.

Press a third of the oat mixture into the bottom of an 8- or 9-inch square baking pan that has been well greased. Smooth on half of the date or apricot mixture. Repeat this again, topping the whole thing with the final third of the oat mixture. Press down firmly so that it all holds together. Bake for 45 minutes or a little less if your oven is fast, until the top layer is nicely browned.

This takes about an hour and a half, including baking.

Banana Coconut Cream Pie Serves 6

Both bananas and coconut milk are used in the treatment of Fluid Dryness constipation, and in general moisten the Yin of the whole body.

| 1 RECIPE OF YOUR FAVORITE PIE CRUST, bottom only |
| 1 box TAPIOCA (you'll need 3 T.) |
| 2 VERY RIPE BANANAS |
| 1 SLICEABLE BANANA |
| 2 T. HONEY (or more to taste) |
| 1 EGG, separated |
| ¼ tsp. SALT |
| 1½ cups COMBINED COCONUT MILK AND CASHEW MILK |
| ¾ tsp. VANILLA EXTRACT |

Crumble Crust Topping

| 5 T. MELTED BUTTER |
| 3 T. HONEY |
| 1½ cups ROLLED OATS or QUICK OATS |
| ½ cup WHOLE WHEAT PASTRY FLOUR |
| ¼ cup WHEAT GERM |
| ¼ tsp. SALT |
| ½ cup SHREDDED UNSWEETENED COCONUT |

Follow the recipe on the Tapioca box, substituting the coconut and cashew milk for the milk and omitting the sugar from the whipped egg white.

To make cashew milk, put ½ cup cashew pieces in a blender and keep adding water as you blend, until you get the consistency and color that you want.

When the pudding is made, mash the two bananas and fold them into the pudding. Place this mixture in a pie shell which is rolled out and fluted at the edges in a 9- to 10-inch pie pan.

Slice the one banana and place the rounds on top of the pudding mixture to cover the whole top. If the banana is small, you may need two to do it.

Sprinkle the crumble crust top on and press it down a bit. Bake for 35 to 45 minutes until the top and crust are browned and golden.

This pie takes one and a half hours to prepare, including baking, and serves six people nicely.

Aduki Bean Brownies   Makes 2 dozen

Aduki beans are a strong diuretic and are a good treatment for edema or Dampness of all types in the body, including Damp Bi conditions. They are not good for anyone with a Fluid Dryness condition.

1 cup UNCOOKED ADUKI BEANS

2 cups APPLE JUICE

1 cup WATER

1 tsp. VANILLA EXTRACT

1 cup PUREED COOKED CHESTNUTS or APPLE SAUCE

½ cup CAROB POWDER

½ cup SWEET RICE or BROWN RICE FLOUR

1 cup SWEET RICE FLOUR

¾ tsp. SALT

½ cup SESAME OIL or ALMOND or PEANUT OIL

½ to 1 cup CHOPPED NUTS (your choice here)

½ to 1 cup RAISINS or DRIED CURRANTS

½ cup BARLEY MALT SYRUP or MAPLE SYRUP (optional)

Rinse aduki beans and soak them 8 hours or overnight. If there is not time for soaking, pressure cook them an extra ten to fifteen minutes. Place the soaked beans in a pressure cooker with water and apple juice and cook under full pressure for 35 to 40 minutes. If you do not have a pressure cooker, boil the beans for 2 hours, checking the liquid level regularly. Preheat oven to 350°.

When beans are soft, mash them until creamy and blend in all other ingredients, adding nuts and dried fruit last. Pour/press the batter (it should be somewhere in between a dough and a batter) into a cake pan or cookie sheet. Spread it out to be ½- to ¾-inch thick. Bake for one hour, a little more or a little less, until the top is dark and firm but still a bit spongy to the touch. Cool for a few minutes and cut into squares. (Note: You can use all sweet rice or all brown rice flour in this recipe, depending upon what is available. Whole wheat flour is also an option, but it will make a much harder brownie and is more cooling to the body.)

This takes 8 hours soaking time, 45 minutes cooking time, 15 minutes to put together, one hour or more to bake and makes about two dozen or a few more squares.

Apple Agar Dessert

This recipe is specifically to cool Hot Lung Syndrome and disperse Phlegm. The Agar cools the lungs, the peaches tone the Qi.

3 BARS AGAR (or 8 T. flakes)
4½ cups APPLE JUICE or PEACH NECTAR (or a mixture)
1½ cups WATER
2 tsp. VANILLA EXTRACT
3 cups PEELED, SLICED PEACHES
2 T. TAHINI
DASH APPLE CIDER VINEGAR
½ tsp. SALT
6 ALMONDS

Bring the agar, juice, salt, and water to a boil. Simmer until dissolved, then stir in the vanilla. Wash and slice the peaches. Line the bottom of a 9-inch shallow baking pan with two-thirds of the peaches. Gently pour the hot agar mixture over the peaches. Chill until firmly set. Whip the remaining peaches with the tahini and vinegar. Use as a sauce over the chilled agar squares. Top with sliced almonds.

Dairyless Pumpkin Pie   Serves 6

By removing the dairy from this classic pie it is a treatment for Dampness in the entire body, specifically the Lungs. It is contraindicated on more than an occasional basis for anyone with Fluid Dryness. This is wonderful for removing Dampness in Lungs and in all Damp Bi Syndromes.

1 RECIPE OF YOUR FAVORITE PIE CRUST (use WHOLE WHEAT pastry flour)

3 cups PUMPKIN PUREE

¾ cup HONEY

¼ tsp. POWDERED CLOVES

3 tsp. CINNAMON

1 tsp. ALLSPICE

¼ to ½ tsp. NUTMEG

1 tsp. SALT

1½ cups SOY MILK or CASHEW MILK

4 EGGS, slightly beaten; or 2 T. KUDZU ROOT POWDER in ½ cup WATER; or 3 T. TAPIOCA, cooked in 1½ cups SOY MILK or CASHEW MILK

(Note: If you decide to use the tapioca instead of the eggs, do NOT use the extra 1½ cups of milk as you would be doubling the amount of liquid that you need. The tapioca does, however, make a very special pie and is very soothing to the Stomach.)

Roll out the pie crust and line a 9- to 10-inch pie pan. Set aside.

Cook all ingredients over a low flame for 15 minutes until it is bubbling slowly but regularly. Then cool slightly and pour into the pie shell and bake for one hour at 300°, then for ¼ hour more at 325° until the crust is golden and the insides filmed over and firm on top. Cool for at least one hour before serving. If you like, whip some cashews with water and honey into a cashew cream as a topping.

Cordials and Liqueurs

As we have described, the line dividing dietary therapy from herbal therapy is an arbitrary one. We have seen that foods are selected according to the same principles and theories as in herbal medicine. In this section we will discuss a number of recipes for herbal liqueurs, cordials, and aperitifs. These can be made by patients in their own homes. They are also an easy way for acupuncturists to become familiar with the use of some major Chinese herbs. Their use can help potentize an acupuncture treatment or make a dietary therapy more effective and specific. Since most are composed of only a single herb their effect is not as far-reaching or comprehensive as an individually tailored, multiple ingredient herbal formula. At the same time, their generalized effect does not require as much knowledge and experience in their use.

Most westerners are at least familiar with the names of several famous European cordials and liqueurs such as Benedictine or Chartreuse. What many of us have forgotten is that they were created by medieval and renaissance herbalists, mostly monastic dwellers, as medicines. "Cordial" means a remedy for the Heart. Unfortunately, the general public has no knowledge of what the ingredients of these liqueurs are, nor for what they were designed to treat. In fact, the formula for Chartreuse is kept as a fast secret with only two persons knowing the formula in its entirety at any given time. The recipes for the following medicinal liqueurs are based on those given by Dr. Sung Hyoun Baek, a traditional medical practitioner from Korea who taught in Chicago.

Alcohol is the first ingredient and the base of each of these recipes. Both patient and practitioner must bear in mind that everything can be thought of as medicine if its energetic nature is understood. Although different types of liqueurs have their own natures depending upon how they are made and with what ingredients, alcohol itself is warm, sweet, pungent and ascending. It enters the Lungs, Stomach, Heart, and Liver meridians. It is Yang and belongs to both Earth and Metal Elements. It assists the Yang, tonifies Qi and Blood, regulates the Qi, expels Cold, removes Blood Stagnation, opens up the meridians, facilitates circulation, and reinforces the actions of herbs combined with it. As such, a *little* liquor is a very valuable medicinal substance. Its use in moderate amounts is indicated in Deficiency syndromes characterized by Cold and diminished circulation.

On the other hand, liquor should not be drunk by those with Liver problems, Hot and/or Damp problems, or simple Excesses. Overconsumption of alcohol will harm the Stomach making it too Hot and will eventually deplete the Stomach Yin. It will harm the Liver and eventually the Heart. It will also cause Dampness to accumulate, which may transform into Glairy Mucous. Since alcohol is also dispersing if too much is taken one is susceptible to invasion by External pathogenic energies (i.e. Liu Yin, or Six Evils). Ejaculation while drunk is particularly debilitating.

Traditionally, medicinal liqueurs are taken in the fall and winter, the time for tonification. They are most often used by middle-aged and older patients who naturally have a tendency to be Deficient in one or more energies. They can be used by others at any time of the year when, due to factors such as debility, fatigue, or trauma, indications of Deficiency are evident. Many tonifying herbs are hard on the digestion and their ingestion with a modicum of alcohol protects the Stomach and the digestive Fire. Younger individuals in good health *should not* use tonifying liqueurs since overtonification will lead to Damp Heat and the generation of complicated and recalcitrant energetic imbalances. This is all too common in America where we tend to think that if a little is good then more must be better. In Chinese medicine this is not the case, particularly with the use of herbs and liqueurs which tonify the sexual energies. Therefore, let the prudent take heed. Healthy young people should not use these tonics unless they have Deficiency dysfunctions as defined by Chinese medicine, not by their own insecurities and peer pressure.

Dr. Sung has suggested the use of vodka as the alcohol base for these recipes. This is because vodka, in his opinion, does not have any additional flavorings or herbal ingredients which might impart their own energies; it is reasonably neutral in terms of the pure energy of alcohol. Vodka is very close to what is called Bai Jiu or White Liquor in Chinese. To two quarts of vodka, Dr. Sung suggests adding approximately one pound of honey in order to sweeten the mixture and make it more digestible. It is also possible to use brandy instead of vodka and honey. Additional sweetening should not be added if brandy is used. Other liquors such as gin should be avoided since the botanicals or herbs in these (in the case of gin, juniper berries) may not be compatible with the herbs to be steeped, nor appropriate for the condition to be treated.

The general procedure in making an herbal tincture is to place the herbs, alcohol, and sweetener (if any) all in a glass jar or ceramic container which is then tightly sealed. This should be put in a cool, dark place such as a cupboard or closet, and left for at least one month. Some herbs require a two month soaking period. Although some herbalists recommend shaking the mixture daily, this is not a hard and fast rule. After the active ingredients have been extracted by the alcohol, the contents can be strained and the medicinal liqueur decanted into another bottle. Dr. T.Y. Pang, in *Chinese Herbal: An Introduction*, also gives a hurry-up method for making a tincture in a shorter period of time. The bottle containing the herbs and alcohol can be placed in a pot of water which has been brought to a boil. The pot should be covered and left to stand until it cools. This procedure is repeated again in three days after which the tincture can be strained and decanted.[25]

Astragalus Liqueur

300 grams ASTRAGALUS (Huang Qi)
2 quarts ALCOHOL
AGE: 1 MONTH
DOSE: 10-60 cc. 3x per day

Functions: Tonifies Yang Qi, stimulates Blood production, stops Deficiency sweating.

Walnut Liqueur

300 grams WALNUTS, macerated in ALCOHOL
AGE: 1 MONTH
DOSE: 60 cc. 3x per day

Functions: tonifies Lungs and Kidneys, tonifies the Jing, transforms Sputum, relieves coughing, relieves Kidney Deficiency lumbago, helps to smooth rough skin.

Red Date Liqueur

600 grams RED DATES (Ta Tsao or Zizyphus sativa)

1 quart ALCOHOL

AGE: 1 MONTH

DOSE: 10-40 cc. 3x per day

Functions: tonifies Yang Qi, stimulates Blood production, aids digestion, tonifies the skin.

Eucommia Liqueur

300 grams EUCOMMIA ULMOIDES (Tu Chung)

2 quarts ALCOHOL

AGE: 1 MONTH

DOSE: 10-60 cc. 3x per day

Functions: tonifies Righteous Qi, tonifies Jing and Kidney Qi, relieves Kidney Deficiency lumbago and soreness in the knees, hypotensive.

Cuscuta Liqueur

300 grams CUSCUTA JAPONICA
(Tu Szu Tzu), preferably smaller seeds

2 quarts ALCOHOL

AGE: 2 MONTHS

DOSE: 10-40 cc. 3x per day

Functions: tonifies Kidneys, relieves Kidney Deficiency lumbago, tonifies Ming Men (Life Gate) Fire, relieves cocks-crow diarrhea.

Ophiopogon Liqueur

300 grams OPHIOPOGON JAPONICUS (Mai Men Tong)

2 quarts ALCOHOL

AGE: 1 MONTH

DOSE: 10-60 cc. 3x per day

Functions: tonifies Kidneys, Heart, Lungs, and Brain, antitussive in Deficiency Yin cough, relieves asthma of Deficient nature, cools Fire of the Heart.

Lycium Liqueur

300 grams LYCIUM CHINENSIS (Kou Chi Tzu)

2 quarts ALCOHOL

AGE: 2 MONTHS

DOSE: 1 to 2 oz. before or after meals

Functions: tonifies Righteous Qi, supports the eyes, muscles, bones, and hormone secretion.

Contraindications: high fever, Excess Damp, weak digestion.

Overconsumption for a prolonged period will damage the Righteous Qi.

Polygonum Liqueur

300 grams POLYGONUM MULTIFLORUM (Ho Shou Wou)

2 quarts ALCOHOL

Cook in a double boiler untile jelly-like

AGE: 1 MONTH

DOSE: 1 to 2 oz. before or after dinner

Functions: stimulates Blood production, tonifies Liver and Kidney Yin, prevents premature greying of hair, tonifies the Jing, calms the Spirit.

Tang Kuei Liqueur

| 300 grams TANG KUEI (Angelica sinensis) |
| 2 quarts ALCOHOL |
| AGE: 1 MONTH |
| DOSE: 10 to 60 cc. 3x per day |

Functions: stimulates Blood production, removes Stagnant Blood, relieves menstrual irregularity and related problems, tonifies Blood Deficiency.

Dioscorea Liqueur

| 300 grams DIOSCOREA JAPONICA (Shan Yao) |
| 2 quarts ALCOHOL |
| AGE: 1 MONTH |
| DOSE: 10-40 cc. 3x per day |

Functions: aids digestion, stops spermatorrhea, stops Deficiency sweating, stops enuresis, tonifies the Kidneys.

Add lemon juice to tonify the Righteous Qi; delete honey or use vodka instead of Brandy in diabetes.

Longan Liqueur

| 300 grams LONGAN (Lung Yan, Euphoria longan) |
| 1 quart ALCOHOL |
| AGE: 1 MONTH |
| DOSE: 10-60 cc. 3x per day |

Functions: mixes Heart and Kidney energy, supports Yin, tonifies Spleen, Stomach and Heart, calms the Spirit, and smoothes the skin.

Overconsumption may cause constipation.

Contraindications: acute infections with localized Stagnant Blood, or severe diarrhea.

Ginseng Liqueur

300 grams GINSENG (Panax genseng)
or TANG SHEN (Codonopsis pilosula)

2 quarts ALCOHOL

AGE: 1 MONTH

DOSE: 10-60 cc. 3x per day

Functions: tonifies both Yin and Yang Qi, stops Deficiency sweating, warms cold limbs, aids digestion, tonifies Qi, and therefore stimulates blood production.

Chinese Quince Liqueur

300 grams CHINESE QUINCE (Mu Gua, Chaenomeles lagenaria)

2 quarts ALCOHOL

AGE: 1 MONTH

DOSE: 10-60 cc. 3x per day

Functions: aids digestion, heats Lower Burner, anti-rheumatic, hypotensive, aids Spleen and Kidney Deficiency diabetes.

All the above liqueurs are made with only a single herbal ingredient. At Chinese apothecaries in Chinatowns across the country, herbal liqueurs are sold based on classical Chinese polypharmacy formulae such as Szechuan Da Bu Chiew, Huku Mugu Chiew, Astragalus Tincture, Shih Chuan Ta Bu Chiew, etc. These are more specific and more powerful tonic wines, use of which should be carefully guided by Chinese medical theory and common clinical practice. Two, three, and more ingredient combinations can be made by the practitioner after they have become more familiar with the theory and practice of Chinese herbalism. Chinese herbs to make the above simple recipes may be purchased by mail from Kwong Sang Lung Company, 947 Grant Avenue, San Francisco, California 94108 or from Chinese American Emporium Limited, 14 Pell Street, New York, New York 10013.

Categorization of Foods

Abalone

Nature:	Neutral
Flavor:	Sweet and salty
Quality:	Yin and Yang
Elemental Quality:	Earth and Water
Treatment Principles:	moistens Yin, clears Heat, benefits semen, sharpens vision

Commonly used in the treatment of cough, leukorrhea, vaginal bleeding, urinary strains, and cataracts.

Contraindications: For those with weak digestion, drink this as a soup.

Aduki Bean

Nature:	Neutral
Flavor:	Sweet and sour taste
Meridian:	Heart and Small Intestine
Quality:	Yin and Yang
Elemental Quality:	Wood and Earth
Treatment Principles:	Tonifies Qi and Blood, tonifies Yin, removes Damp, harmonizes Blood, heals swelling, counteracts toxins, reduces weight

Commonly used in the treatment of edema, diarrhea, beriberi, jaundice, anal hemorrhage, and carbuncle.

Contraindications: Deficiency of Fluids and emaciation

Agar

Nature:	Cold
Flavor:	Sweet
Meridian:	Sliding
Direction:	Lung and Liver
Quality:	Yin and Yang
Elemental Quality:	Earth and Water
Treatment Principles:	Removes Floating Heat in Upper Burner, clears the Lungs

Commonly used in the treatment of hemorrhoids.

Contraindications: Spleen Yang and Kidney Yang Deficiency

Alfalfa

Nature:	Neutral
Flavor:	Bitter
Quality:	Yin
Elemental Quality:	Fire
Treatment Principles:	Dries Damp, clears Spleen and Stomach, benefits Small and Large Intestine, removes Bladder stones

Commonly used in treatment of Bladder stones and edema.

Almond

Nature:	Neutral
Flavor:	Sweet
Meridian:	Lungs
Quality:	Yang
Elemental Quality:	Earth
Treatment Principles:	Tonifies Qi and Blood, lubricates Lungs, relieves cough, transforms Sputum, lowers Rebellious Qi

Commonly used in treatment of cough.

Contraindications: Damp Sputum

Amasake (Fermented glutinous rice)

Nature:	Warm
Flavor:	Sweet
Meridian:	Lungs
Quality:	Yang
Elemental Quality:	Earth and Metal
Treatment Principles:	Assists Yang, regulates, tonifies, and benefits Qi, tonifies Blood, removes Blood Stagnation, expels Cold, produces Fluids, activates Blood

Anchovy

Nature:	Warm
Flavor:	Sweet
Quality:	Yang
Elemental Quality:	Earth
Treatment Principles:	Assists Yang, tonifies Yang, tonifies Qi and Blood, expels Cold, appetant, lactogogue

Commonly used in treatment of agalactia, edema, and dysuria.

Apple

Nature:	Cool
Flavor:	Sweet
Direction:	Descending
Quality:	Yin and Yang
Elemental Quality:	Earth
Treatment Principles:	Tonifies Qi and Blood, clears Heat, sedates Yang, produces Fluids, lubricates Lungs, removes mental depression, relieves Summer Heat, appetant

Asparagus

Nature:	Cold
Flavor:	Sweet and bitter
Meridian:	Lungs and Kidneys
Direction:	Descending and Ascending
Quality:	Yin and Yang
Elemental Quality:	Fire and Earth
Treatment Principles:	Tonifies Qi and Blood, clears Heat, dries Damp, diaphoretic, tonifies Yin, lubricates Dryness, clears the Lungs, sedates Fire

Commonly used in the treatment of hemoptysis, pulmonary tuberculosis, chronic bronchitis, diabetes, and constipation.

Contraindications: Deficiency Cold diarrhea, and Wind Cold cough

Bamboo Shoots

Nature:	Cold
Flavor:	Sweet
Direction:	Descending
Quality:	Yin and Yang
Elemental Quality:	Earth
Treatment Principles:	Tonifies Qi and Blood, clears Heat, tonifies Yin, counteracts toxins

Commonly used in treatment of measles.

Contraindications: Spleen Deficiency

Banana

Nature:	Cold
Flavor:	Sweet
Direction:	Descending
Elemental Quality:	Earth
Treatment Principles:	Tonifies Qi and Blood, clears Heat, tones Yin, lubricates intestines, counteracts toxins

Commonly used in treatment of thirst, constipation, bleeding piles and alcoholism.

Barley

Nature:	Cool
Flavor:	Sweet and salty
Meridian:	Stomach and Spleen
Direction:	Descending
Quality:	Yin and Yang
Elemental Quality:	Earth and Water
Treatment Principles:	Tonifies Qi and Blood, clears Heat, sedates Yang, lubricates Dryness, tonifies Yin, harmonizes Stomach, expands Intestines

Commonly used in treatment of diarrhea, edema, dysuria, and indigestion.

Basil

Nature:	Warm
Flavor:	Pungent
Meridian:	Stomach and Spleen
Direction:	Ascending
Quality:	Yang
Elemental Quality:	Metal
Treatment Principles:	Assists Yang, tonifies and regulates Qi, removes Blood Stagnation, expels Cold, sedates Yin, disperses Wind, promotes flow of Qi, transforms Damp, activates the Blood, counteracts toxins

Commonly used in the treatment of headache of external etiology, abdominal swelling, abdominal pain, menstrual irregularity, diarrhea, contusions, pruritis, skin eruptions, and belching.

Contraindications: Qi Deficiency and Dry Blood

Bay Leaf

Nature:	Warm
Flavor:	Pungent
Direction:	Ascending
Quality:	Yang
Elemental Quality:	Metal
Treatment Principles:	Assists Yang, regulates and tonifies Qi, removes Blood Stagnation, expels Cold, sedates Yin

Commonly used in the treatment of childrens' skin eruptions (particularly behind the ear) and pruritis.

Beef

Nature:	Neutral
Flavor:	Sweet
Meridian:	Large Intestine, Stomach, Spleen
Quality:	Yang
Elemental Quality:	Earth
Treatment Principles:	Tones Qi and Blood, tonifies Yin, tonifies Stomach/Spleen, strengthens tendons and bones

Commonly used in treatment of emaciation, edema, diabetes, Yin Deficiency, low back pain, and weak knees.

Beef Liver

Nature:	Neutral
Flavor:	Sweet
Direction:	Ascending
Quality:	Yang
Elemental Quality:	Earth
Treatment Principles:	Tonifies Qi and Blood, tonifies Liver, sharpens vision

Commonly used in treatment of optic nerve atrophy and night blindness.

Beet

Nature:	Neutral
Flavor:	Sweet
Quality:	Yang
Elemental Quality:	Earth
Treatment Principles:	Tonifies Qi and Blood, tonifies Yin, opens Meridians, lowers Rebellious Qi, expands the chest

Black Fungus

Nature:	Neutral
Flavor:	Sweet
Meridian:	Large Intestine and Stomach
Direction:	Ascending
Quality:	Yang
Elemental Quality:	Earth
Treatment Principles:	Tonifies Qi and Blood, cools the Blood, arrests bleeding

Commonly used in treatment of hematuria, vaginal bleeding, hemorrhoids, watering eyes, and toothache.

Contraindications: watery stools

Black Pepper

Nature:	Hot
Flavor:	Pungent
Direction:	Ascending and Floating
Quality:	Yang
Elemental Quality:	Metal
Treatment Principles:	Assists Yang, regulates Qi, benefits Qi, removes Blood Stagnation, expels Cold, warms Middle Burner, lowers Rebellious Qi, eliminates Sputum, counteracts toxins

Commonly used in treatment of Cold Sputum, indigestion, Cold abdominal pain, vomiting clear liquid, Cold diarrhea, food poisoning, toothache due to Wind, nephritis, neurasthenia, and skin diseases.

Contraindications: Yin Deficiency and Internal Heat (considered toxic)

Black Sesame

Nature:	Neutral
Flavor:	Sweet
Meridian:	Kidneys and Liver
Direction:	Ascending
Quality:	Yang
Elemental Quality:	Earth
Treatment Principles:	Tonifies Qi and Blood, tones Liver and Kidneys, lubricates the 5 Zang (solid organs)

Commonly used in the treatment of vertigo, rheumatism, paralysis, constipation, premature gray hair, and agalactia.

Contraindications: Spleen Deficiency and watery stools

Black Soybean

Nature:	Neutral
Flavor:	Sweet
Meridian:	Spleen and Kidneys
Direction:	Ascending
Quality:	Yang
Elemental Quality:	Earth
Treatment Principles:	Tonifies Qi and Blood, activates the Blood, benefits Water, expels Wind, counteracts toxins

Commonly used in the treatment of edema, Wind Bi (rheumatism), jaundice, beriberi, and spasms.

Brown Sugar

Nature:	Warm
Flavor:	Sweet
Meridian:	Spleen and Liver
Quality:	Yang
Elemental Quality:	Earth
Treatment Principles:	Assists Yang, tonifies Qi and Blood, benefits Qi, removes Stagnant Blood, expels Cold, sedates Yin, tonifies the Middle Burner, relaxes the Liver, activates the Blood, dissolves coagulations

Commonly used in the treatment of postpartum suppression of lochia, thirst, vomiting, belching, and dysentery.

Contraindications: Damp Sputum

Buckwheat (Kasha)

Nature:	Cool
Flavor:	Sweet
Meridian:	Large Intestine, Stomach, Spleen
Direction:	Descending
Quality:	Yin and Yang
Elemental Quality:	Earth
Treatment Principles:	Tonifies Qi and Blood, clears Heat, sedates Yang, improves appetite, expands intestines, lowers Rebellious Qi, eliminates accumulations

Commonly used in treatment of carbuncle, scrofula, burns, erysipelas, and chronic diarrhea.

Contraindications: vertigo, indigestion, or Wind or Hot diseases

Butter

Nature:	Warm
Flavor:	Sweet
Quality:	Yang
Elemental Quality:	Earth
Treatment Principles:	Assists Yang, tonifies Qi and Blood, removes Stagnant Blood, expels Cold, sedates Yin

Commonly used in treatment of scabies, skin eruption, and body odor.

Excessive consumption may reactivate a latent disease.

Cabbage

Nature:	Neutral
Flavor:	Sweet
Meridian:	Large Intestine, Stomach
Direction:	Ascending
Quality:	Yang
Elemental Quality:	Earth
Treatment Principles:	Tones Qi and Blood, relieves mental depression, promotes digestion

Commonly used in treatment of Hot cough, constipation, and erysipelas.

Contraindications: Qi Deficiency, Stomach Yang Deficiency, and nausea

Capers

Nature:	Warm
Flavor:	Pungent and bitter
Direction:	Ascending
Quality:	Yang
Elemental Quality:	Metal
Treatment Principles:	Assists Yang, regulates and tonifies Qi, sedates Yin, expels Cold, removes Stagnant Blood, expels Wind, removes Damp

Commonly used in the treatment of rheumatoid arthritis.

Carambola (Star Fruit)

Nature:	Cold
Flavor:	Sweet and sour
Direction:	Ascending
Quality:	Yin and Yang
Elemental Quality:	Wood and Earth
Treatment Principles:	Tonifies Qi and Blood, clears Heat, tones Yin, produces Fluids, counteracts toxins

Commonly used in treatment of cough, thirst, stomatitis, and toothache.

Contraindications: Stomach/Spleen Yang Deficiency

Carrot

Nature:	Neutral
Flavor:	Sweet
Meridian:	Lungs, spleen
Direction:	Ascending
Quality:	Yang
Elemental Quality:	Earth
Treatment Principles:	Strengthens Spleen, transforms accumulations

Commonly used in treatment of indigestion, chronic dysentery, cough, measles, pertussis, and chicken pox.

Cayenne

Nature:	Hot
Flavor:	Pungent
Meridian:	Spleen, Heart
Direction:	Ascending
Quality:	Yang
Elemental Quality:	Metal
Treatment Principles:	Assists Yang, regulates Qi, removes Blood Stagnation, expels Cold, sedates Yin, warms Middle Burner, appetant, digestant

Commonly used in treatment of Cold abdominal pain, vomiting, diarrhea, and chilblains.

Contraindications: Yin Deficiency, Excessive Fire, cough, or eye disease

Celery

Nature:	Cool
Flavor:	Sweet and bitter
Meridian:	Stomach, Liver
Direction:	Descending
Quality:	Yin and Yang
Elemental Quality:	Fire and Earth
Treatment Principles:	Tonifies Qi and Blood, clears heat, sedates Yang, dries Damp, diaphoretic, calms Liver, expels Wind

Commonly used in treatment of essential hypertension, vertigo, headache, conjunctivitis, flushing, hematuria, and carbuncle.

Contraindications: scabies

Cheese

Nature:	Neutral
Flavor:	Sweet and Sour
Direction:	Ascending and Descending
Quality:	Yin and Yang
Elemental Quality:	Wood and Earth
Treatment Principles:	Tonifies Qi and Blood, tonifies Lungs, lubricates intestines, nourishes Yin, quenches thirst

Commonly used in treatment of Deficiency fever, thirst, Dry Intestine constipation, dry skin, skin eruptions, and pruritis.

Contraindications: weak digestion

Cherry

Nature:	Warm
Flavor:	Sweet, Harsh
Quality:	Yang
Elemental Quality:	Earth
Treatment Principles:	Assists Yang, tones Qi and blood, benefits Qi, removes Blood Stagnation, expels Cold, sedates Yin, expels Wind Damp

Commonly used in the treatment of paralysis, numbness in the four extremities, chilblains, and rheumatic pain in the lower half of the body.

Contraindications: vomiting

Chestnut

Nature:	Warm
Flavor:	Sweet
Meridian:	Spleen and Kidneys
Quality:	Yang
Elemental Quality:	Earth
Treatment Principles:	Assists Yang, tonifies Qi and Blood, benefits Qi, removes Stagnant Blood, expels Cold, sedates Yin, nourishes Stomach/Spleen, tonifies Kidneys, strengthens tendons, activates Blood

Commonly used in the treatment of nausea, weak low back and knees, hemoptysis, hemorrhage, fractures and contusions, and scrofula.

Chicken

Nature:	Warm
Flavor:	Sweet
Meridian:	Stomach, Spleen
Quality:	Yang
Elemental Quality:	Earth
Treatment Principles:	Assists Yang, tonifies Qi and Blood, benefits Qi, removes Blood Stagnation, expels Cold, sedates Yin, warms Middle Burner, tonifies the Jing, fills the Marrow

Commonly used in the treatment of anorexia, diarrhea, dysentery, diabetes, edema, polyuria, vaginal bleeding, leukorrhea, and agalactia.

Contraindications: Excess diseases or External diseases

Chicken Egg

Nature:	Neutral
Flavor:	Sweet
Direction:	Ascending
Quality:	Yin and Yang
Elemental Quality:	Earth
Treatment Principles:	Tones Qi and Blood, lubricates Dryness, tones Yin, secures the fetus

Commonly used in the treatment of Dry cough, conjunctivitis, sore throat, "fetus in motion," postpartum thirst, diarrhea, and burns.

Contraindications: Wind diseases

Chicken Gizzard

Nature:	Neutral
Flavor:	Sweet
Meridian:	Stomach, Spleen
Elemental Quality:	Earth and Water
Treatment Principles:	Tonifies Qi and Blood, eliminates accumulations, tones Stomach/Spleen

Commonly used in treatment of indigestion, vomiting, diarrhea, malnutrition, diabetes, enuresis, sore throat, and polyuria.

Chicken Liver

Nature:	Warm
Flavor:	Sweet
Meridian:	Kidney and Liver
Quality:	Yang
Elemental Quality:	Earth
Treatment Principles:	Assists Yang, tonifies Qi and Blood, benefits Qi, removes Blood Stagnation, expels Cold, sedates Yin, tonifies Liver and Kidneys

Commonly used in treatment of blurred vision, juvenile malnutrition, impotence, menstrual flow in pregnancy, and enuresis.

Clam

Nature:	Cold
Flavor:	Salty
Meridian:	Stomach
Direction:	Sinking
Quality:	Yin
Elemental Quality:	Water
Treatment Principles:	Clears Heat, lubricates Dryness, tonifies Yin, transforms Sputum, softens hardness

Commonly used in the treatment of diabetes, edema, Sputum accumulation, scrofula, vaginal bleeding, leukorrhea, and hemorrhoids.

Coconut Meat

Nature:	Neutral
Flavor:	Sweet
Direction:	Ascending
Quality:	Yang
Elemental Quality:	Earth
Treatment Principles:	Tonifies Qi and Blood, expels Wind

Commonly used in the treatment of malnutrition in children.

Coconut Milk

Nature:	Warm
Flavor:	Sweet
Quality:	Yang
Elemental Quality:	Earth
Treatment Principles:	Tonifies Qi and Blood, assists Yang, benefits Qi, removes Blood Stagnation, expels Cold, sedates Yin, clears Summer Heat, quenches thirst, waters Yin

Commonly used in the treatment of diabetes, hemoptysis, and edema.

Contraindications: Qi Deficiency

Corn

Nature:	Neutral
Flavor:	Sweet
Meridian:	Large Intestine and Stomach
Quality:	Yang
Elemental Quality:	Earth
Treatment Principles:	Tonifies Qi and Blood, regulates Middle Burner, appetant, diuretic

Commonly used in the treatment of Heart disease and sexual weakness.

Coriander

Nature:	Warm
Flavor:	Pungent
Meridian:	Lungs and Spleen
Direction:	Ascending
Quality:	Yang
Elemental Quality:	Metal
Treatment Principles:	Regulates Qi, expels Cold, removes Blood Stagnation, sedates Yin, diaphoretic, facilitates eruption of measles, promotes digestion, lowers Rebellious Qi

Commonly used in the treatment of indigestion and prolonged incubation of measles.

Contraindications: after measles have already erupted

Crab

Nature:	Cold
Flavor:	Salty
Meridian:	Stomach
Direction:	Sinking
Quality:	Yin
Elemental Quality:	Water
Treatment Principles:	Clears Heat, lubricates Dryness, tonifies Yin, removes Stagnant Blood, reconnects fractured bones

Commonly used in the treatment of fractures, poison ivy, and burns

Contraindications: Wind disease, Stomach Yang Deficiency, recuperation from External disease. Considered toxic; overconsumption is not advised.

Cucumber

Nature:	Cool
Flavor:	Sweet
Meridian:	Large Intestine, Stomach, Spleen
Direction:	Descending
Quality:	Yin and Yang
Elemental Quality:	Earth
Treatment Principles:	Tonifies Qi and Blood, clears Heat, sedates Yang, benefits Water, counteracts toxins

Commonly used in the treatment of thirst, mental depression, sore throat, conjunctivitis, and burns.

Contraindications: Cold Sputum disease, abdominal pain, and diarrhea

Day Lily Flower

Nature:	Cool
Flavor:	Sweet
Direction:	Descending
Quality:	Yin and Yang
Treatment Principles:	Tones Qi and Blood, clears Heat, sedates Yang, benefits Damp Heat, expands chest and diaphragm

Commonly used in the treatment of dysuria, hematuria, jaundice, chest congestion, insomnia, and bleeding hemorrhoids.

Dill Seed

Nature:	Warm
Flavor:	Pungent
Meridian:	Spleen and Kidneys
Direction:	Ascending
Quality:	Yang
Elemental Quality:	Metal
Treatment Principles:	Assists Yang, tones Qi, regulates the Qi, removes Blood Stagnation, expels Cold, sedates Yin, warms the Spleen and Kidneys

Commonly used in the treatment of vomiting, hiccough, anorexia, Cold abdominal pain, and Cold hernia.

Contraindications: Yin Deficiency with False Fire Flaring

Duck

Nature:	Neutral
Flavor:	Sweet
Meridian:	Lungs and Kidneys
Direction:	Ascending
Quality:	Yin and Yang
Elemental Quality:	Earth
Treatment Principles:	Tonifies Qi and Blood, lubricates Dryness, tones Yin, nourishes the Stomach, heals swelling

Commonly used in the treatment of hot sensations in the body, edema, and cough.

Contraindications: If Spleen Deficiency and hemorrhage, overconsumption may cause Stagnant Qi.

Eggplant

Nature:	Cool
Flavor:	Sweet
Meridian:	Large Intestine, Stomach, and Spleen
Direction:	Descending
Quality:	Yin and Yang
Elemental Quality:	Earth
Treatment Principles:	Tonifies Qi and Blood, clears Heat, sedates Yang, removes Stagnant Blood, relieves pain, heals swelling

Commonly used in the treatment of anal hemorrhage, carbuncle, skin ulcer, and mastitis.

Contraindications: Overconsumption may injure the Uterus in a woman without Stagnant Blood.

Fennel Seed

Nature:	Warm
Flavor:	Pungent
Meridian:	Stomach, Bladder, and Kidneys
Direction:	Ascending
Quality:	Yang
Treatment Principles:	Tonifies the Yang, tonifies the Qi, regulates the Qi, removes Blood Stagnation, expels Cold, sedates Yin, warms the Kidneys, harmonizes the Stomach

Commonly used in the treatment of Cold "hernia," Cold lower abdominal pain, lumbago, stomachache, and vomiting.

Contraindications: Yin Deficiency with False Fire Flaring

Fig

Nature:	Neutral
Flavor:	Sweet
Meridian:	Lungs, Large Intestine, Spleen
Direction:	Ascending
Quality:	Yang
Elemental Quality:	Earth
Treatment Principles:	Tonifies Qi and Blood, strengthens the Stomach, clears the intestines, heals swelling, counteracts toxins

Commonly used in the treatment of enteritis, constipation, dysentery, hemorrhoids, pharyngitis, and carbuncles.

Garlic

Nature:	Warm
Flavor:	Pungent
Meridian:	Lungs, Stomach, Spleen
Direction:	Ascending
Quality:	Yang
Elemental Quality:	Metal
Treatment Principles:	Assists Yang, tones and regulates the Qi, removes Blood Stagnation, expels Cold, sedates Yin, promotes the flow of sluggish Qi, warms the Stomach/Spleen, eliminates abdominal obstruction, counteracts toxins, destroys worms

Commonly used in the treatment of indigestion, Cold stomachache, diarrhea, edema, dysentery, malaria, pertussis, pulmonary tuberculosis, pneumonia, snake bite, and hepatitis.

Contraindications: Yin Deficiency with False Fire Flaring, eye diseases, canker sores; tooth, tongue, or throat diseases

157

Ginger (dried)

Nature:	Hot
Flavor:	Pungent
Meridian:	Lungs, Stomach, Spleen
Direction:	Ascending
Quality:	Yang
Elemental Quality:	Metal
Treatment Principles:	Assists Yang, regulates and benefits the Qi, removes Blood Stagnation, expels Cold, sedates Yin, warms the Middle Burner, opens the meridians

Commonly used in the treatment of Cold stomachache, vomiting, diarrhea, cold hands and feet, rheumatism, morning sickness, epistaxis, and watery diarrhea.

Contraindications: Yin Deficiency, Internal Heat or Hot Blood hemorrhaging

Ginger (fresh)

Nature:	Warm
Flavor:	Pungent
Meridian:	Lungs, Stomach, Spleen
Direction:	Ascending
Quality:	Yang
Elemental Quality:	Metal
Treatment Principles:	Assists Yang, regulates, benefits and tonifies the Qi, removes Blood Stagnation, expels Cold, sedates Yin, improves Sputum conditions, alleviates vomiting, diaphoretic

Commonly used in the treatment of the common cold, vomiting, sputum, cough, diarrhea, rheumatism, and acute orchitis.

Contraindications: Yin Deficiency and Internal Heat

Gluten (Seitan)

Nature:	Cool
Flavor:	Sweet
Direction:	Descending
Quality:	Yin and Yang
Elemental Quality:	Earth
Treatment Principles:	Tonifies Qi and Blood, clears Heat, sedates Yang, harmonizes Middle Burner, reduces fever, quenches thirst

Goose

Nature:	Neutral
Flavor:	Sweet
Meridian:	Lungs, Spleen
Elemental Quality:	Earth
Treatment Principles:	Tonifies Qi and Blood, benefits Qi, harmonizes Stomach, relieves diarrhea

Commonly used in the treatment of diabetes.

Contraindications: Damp Heat

Grapes

Nature:	Neutral
Flavor:	Sweet and Sour
Meridian:	Lungs, Spleen, Kidneys
Direction:	Ascending and Descending
Quality:	Yin and Yang
Elemental Quality:	Wood and Earth
Treatment Principles:	Tonifies Qi and Blood, strengthens tendons and bones, promotes diuresis, tonifies the Will

Commonly used in treatment of Deficiency cough, palpitations, night sweat, rheumatism, edema, and excessive appetite.

Excessive consumption will cause blurred vision.

Herring

Nature:	Neutral
Flavor:	Sweet
Meridian:	Lungs and Spleen
Direction:	Ascending
Quality:	Yang
Elemental Quality:	Earth
Treatment Principles:	Tonifies the Qi and Blood, tonifies Deficiency, warms the Middle Burner, lubricates Dryness, analgesic, counteracts toxins

Commonly used in treatment of Deficiency fatigue.

Contraindications: skin eruptions or when recovering from a chronic disease

Honey

Nature:	Neutral
Flavor:	Sweet
Meridian:	Lungs, Large Intestine, Spleen
Direction:	Ascending
Quality:	Yang
Elemental Quality:	Earth
Treatment Principles:	Tonifies Qi and Blood, tonifies the Middle Burner, lubricates Dryness, analgesic, counteracts toxins

Commonly used in treatment of Dry cough, constipation, stomachache, sinusitis, canker sores, burns, and aconite poisoning.

Contraindications: Sputum Damp diseases, congestion of the Middle Burner or diarrhea (due to its sliding nature)

Job's Tears (Coix lachryma)

Nature:	Cool
Flavor:	Sweet and Neutral
Meridian:	Lungs, Large Intestine, Stomach, Spleen, Kidneys
Direction:	Descending
Quality:	Yin and Yang
Elemental Quality:	Earth
Treatment Principles:	Tones Qi and Blood, seeps Damp, diuretic, clears Heat, sedates Yang, strengthens Spleen, tonifies the Lungs

Commonly used in treatment of edema and beriberi.

Kelp

Nature:	Cold
Flavor:	Salty
Meridian:	Stomach and Spleen
Direction:	Sinking
Quality:	Yin
Elemental Quality:	Water
Treatment Principles:	Clears Heat, lubricates Dryness, tones Yin, softens Hardness, promotes flow of Water

Commonly used in the treatment of scrofula, goiter, edema, dysphagia, orchitis, and leukorrhea.

Contraindications: Stomach and Spleen Yang Deficiencies or Stomach/Spleen Dampness

Kidney Bean

Nature:	Neutral
Flavor:	Sweet and neutral
Quality:	Yang
Elemental Quality:	Earth
Treatment Principles:	Tonifies Qi and Blood, tonifies Yin, clears Heat, diuretic, heals swelling

Commonly used in the treatment of edema and beriberi.

Kohlrabi

Flavor:	Pungent, sweet, bitter
Direction:	Ascending
Quality:	Yin and Yang
Elemental Quality:	Fire, Earth, and Metal
Treatment Principles:	Assists Yang, benefits and regulates the Qi, tones the Qi and Blood, dries Damp, diaphoretic, removes Stagnant Blood, expels Cold, sedates Yin

Commonly used in treatment of dysuria, hemafecia, swelling sinusitis, and swelling of scrotum.

Contraindications: During convalescence or with skin eruptions, overconsumption will harm both Qi and Blood.

Kudzu Root Powder

Flavor:	Sweet
Meridian:	Stomach
Direction:	Descending
Quality:	Yin and Yang
Elemental Quality:	Earth
Treatment Principles:	Tones Qi and Blood, clears Heat, tones Yin, produces Fluid, quenches thirst, relieves mental depression

Commonly used in treatment of thirst, Hot skin eruptions, sore throat, toothache, and hangover.

Lamb Kidney

Nature:	Warm
Flavor:	Sweet
Quality:	Yang
Elemental Quality:	Earth
Treatment Principles:	Assists Yang, tones Qi and Blood, expels Cold, sedates Yin, removes Qi and Blood Stagnation, tonifies the Kidneys, benefits the Jing (Essence) and Marrow

Commonly used in treatment of fatigue, low back and spine pain, diabetes, polyuria, weak legs and knees, deafness, impotence, and enuresis.

Lamb's Quarters

Nature:	Neutral
Flavor:	Sweet
Direction:	Ascending
Quality:	Yang
Elemental Quality:	Earth
Treatment Principles:	Tones Qi and Blood, clears Heat, benefits Damp, vermifuge

Commonly used in the treatment of dysentery, diarrhea, eczema, and insect bites.

Considered a minor toxin.

Leek

Nature:	Warm
Flavor:	Pungent, harsh
Direction:	Ascending and Descending
Quality:	Yin and Yang
Elemental Quality:	Wood and Metal
Treatment Principles:	Assists Yang, tones, regulates and benefits the Qi, removes Stagnant Blood, expels Cold, sedates Yin, removes Stomach Heat

Commonly used in the treatment of diarrhea, hemorrhage, and dysphagia.

Lettuce

Nature:	Cool
Flavor:	Sweet and Bitter
Meridian:	Large Intestine and Stomach
Direction:	Descending
Quality:	Yin and Yang
Elemental Quality:	Fire and Earth
Treatment Principles:	Tones Qi and Blood, clears Heat, sedates Yang, dries Dampness, diuretic

Commonly used in the treatment of oliguria, hematuria, and agalactia.

Contraindications: eye diseases; overconsumption may cause blurred vision.

162

Litchi

Nature:	Warm
Flavor:	Sweet and Sour
Meridian:	Spleen and Liver
Direction:	Descending
Quality:	Yin and Yang
Elemental Quality:	Wood and Earth
Treatment Principles:	Assists Yang, tones Qi and Blood, benefits Qi, removes Blood Stagnation, expels Cold, sedates Yin, produces Fluids, regulates Qi, analgesic

Commonly used in the treatment of hiccough, thirst, stomachache, scrofula, toothache, and senile cocks-crow diarrhea.

Contraindications: Yin Deficiency and Internal Heat

Longan

Nature:	Warm
Flavor:	Sweet
Meridian:	Spleen and Heart
Elemental Quality:	Earth
Treatment Principles:	Assists Yang, tones Qi and Blood, benefits Qi, removes Blood Stagnation, expels Cold, sedates Yin, benefits Heart and Spleen, secures the Spirit

Commonly used in the treatment of weakness, insomnia, convulsion, amnesia, and nervous excitability.

Contraindications: Glairy Mucous or Dampness

Lotus Root

Nature:	Cold
Flavor:	Sweet
Meridian:	Stomach, Spleen, Heart
Direction:	Descending
Quality:	Yin and Yang
Elemental Quality:	Earth
Treatment Principles:	Tonifies Qi and Blood, clears Heat, tones Yin, cools Blood (when fresh), tones Spleen, appetant, tones Blood, produces muscles, relieves diarrhea (when cooked)

Fresh root is commonly used in the treatment of thirst, hemoptysis, epistaxis, and dysuria. Cooked root is commonly used in the treatment of anorexia and diarrhea.

Lotus Seed

Nature:	Neutral
Flavor:	Sweet, harsh
Meridian:	Spleen, Heart, Kidneys
Direction:	Ascending
Quality:	Yang
Elemental Quality:	Earth
Treatment Principles:	Tones Qi and Blood, nourishes the Heart, tones the Kidneys, tones the Spleen, constricts the Intestines

Commonly used in the treatment of dream-disturbed sleep, spermatorrhea, dysuria, Deficiency diarrhea, and vaginal bleeding.

Contraindications: congestion of Middle Burner or Fluid Deficiency diarrhea

Mackerel (tuna)

Nature:	Neutral
Flavor:	Sweet
Meridian:	Stomach
Direction:	Ascending
Quality:	Yang
Elemental Quality:	Earth
Treatment Principles:	Tonifies Qi and Blood, transforms Damp, benefits Qi

Commonly used in the treatment of beriberi and Damp Bi (rheumatism).

Malt Sugar

Nature:	Warm
Flavor:	Sweet
Meridian:	Lungs, Stomach, Spleen
Quality:	Yang
Elemental Quality:	Earth
Treatment Principles:	Assists Yang, tonifies Qi and Blood, benefits Qi, removes Stagnant Blood, expels Cold, sedates Yin, relaxes the Middle Burner, produces Fluid, lubricates Dryness

Commonly used in the treatment of tenesmus, abdominal pain, Dry cough, hemoptysis, thirst, sore throat, and constipation.

Mango

Nature:	Cold
Flavor:	Sweet and Sour
Direction:	Descending
Quality:	Yin and Yang
Elemental Quality:	Wood and Earth
Treatment Principles:	Tones Qi and Blood, clears Heat, sedates Yang, benefits Stomach, relieves vomiting, quenches thirst, diuretic

Commonly used in the treatment of cough, thirst, and Lung disease.

Contraindications: With common cold, indigestion, polyuria or during convalescence, overconsumption may cause itching or skin eruptions.

Marjoram

Nature:	Cool
Flavor:	Pungent
Direction:	Ascending
Quality:	Yin and Yang
Elemental Quality:	Metal
Treatment Principles:	Assists Yang, tones the Blood, benefits the Qi, removes Blood Stagnation, diaphoretic, transforms Damp

Commonly used in the treatment of the common cold, fever, vomiting, chest congestion, diarrhea, jaundice, rickets in children, pruritis, and leukorrhea.

Milk

Nature:	Neutral
Flavor:	Sweet
Meridian:	Lungs, Stomach, Heart
Direction:	Ascending
Quality:	Yang
Elemental Quality:	Earth
Treatment Principles:	Tonifies Qi and Blood, tonifies Deficiency, benefits Lungs and Stomach, produces Fluids, lubricates intestines

Commonly used in the treatment of indigestion, dysphagia, diabetes, and constipation.

Contraindications: Stomach/Spleen Yang Deficiency, Sputum Damp, or diarrhea

Millet

Nature:	Cool
Flavor:	Sweet and Salty
Meridian:	Stomach, Spleen, and Kidneys
Direction:	Descending
Quality:	Yin and Yang
Elemental Quality:	Earth and Water
Treatment Principles:	Tones Qi and Blood, clears Heat, sedates Yang, lubricates Dryness, tones Yin, harmonizes the Middle Burner, benefits the Kidneys, counteracts toxins

Commonly used in the treatment of indigestion, vomiting, diarrhea, and diabetes.

Contraindications: Stomach/Spleen Yang Deficiency

Mulberry

Nature:	Cold
Flavor:	Sweet
Meridian:	Kidneys and Liver
Direction:	Descending
Quality:	Yin and Yang
Elemental Quality:	Earth
Treatment Principles:	Tonifies Qi and Blood, clears Heat, tones Yin, tonifies Liver, benefits Kidneys, stops Wind

Commonly used in the treatment of diabetes, constipation, blurred vision, tinnitus, scrofula, difficulty in flexing and extending the joints, and insomnia.

Mung Bean

Nature:	Cool
Flavor:	Sweet
Meridian:	Stomach and Heart
Direction:	Descending
Quality:	Yin and Yang
Elemental Quality:	Earth
Treatment Principles:	Tonifies Qi and Blood, clears Heat, sedates Yang, tones Yin, counteracts toxins, relieves Summer Heat

Commonly used in the treatment of edema, diarrhea, erysipelas, carbuncle, diabetes, dysuria, mumps, burns, and lead poisoning.

Mung Bean Sprouts

Nature:	Cold
Flavor:	Sweet
Quality:	Yin and Yang
Elemental Quality:	Earth
Treatment Principles:	Tonifies Qi and Blood, clears Heat, tones Yin, counteracts toxins, benefits the Triple Heater

Commonly used in the treatment of alcoholism.

Contraindications: Stomach/Spleen Yang Deficiency

Mushroom (Common button)

Nature:	Cool
Flavor:	Sweet
Meridian:	Lungs, Large Intestine, Stomach, Spleen
Direction:	Descending
Quality:	Yin and Yang
Elemental Quality:	Earth
Treatment Principles:	Tonifies Qi and Blood, clears Heat, sedates Yang, calms Spirit, appetant, regulates Qi, transforms Sputum

Commonly used in the treatment of vomiting and diarrhea.

Overconsumption may disturb the Qi.

Musk Melon

Nature:	Cold
Flavor:	Sweet
Meridian:	Stomach and Heart
Direction:	Descending
Quality:	Yin and Yang
Elemental Quality:	Earth
Treatment Principles:	Tonifies Qi and Blood, clears Heat, tones Yin, relieves Summer Heat, relieves mental depression, quenches thirst, diuretic

Commonly used in the treatment of dysuria.

Contraindications: Stomach/Spleen Yang Deficiency with abdominal swelling or watery stools

Mussel

Nature:	Warm
Flavor:	Salty
Meridian:	Kidneys and Liver
Quality:	Yin and Yang
Elemental Quality:	Water
Treatment Principles:	Assists Yang, tones Qi, lubricates Dryness, benefits Qi, removes Blood Stagnation, expels Cold, sedates Yin, tonifies Liver and Kidneys, benefits Jing and Blood

Commonly used in the treatment of goiter, vertigo, night sweats, impotence, lumbago, vaginal bleeding, leukorrhea, and abdominal obstruction and swelling.

Mustard Greens

Nature:	Warm
Flavor:	Pungent
Meridian:	Lungs
Direction:	Ascending
Quality:	Yang
Elemental Quality:	Metal
Treatment Principles:	Assists Yang, tones, regulates and benefits the Qi, removes Blood Stagnation, expels Cold, sedates Yin, expands the Lungs, expels Sputum, warms the Middle Burner

Commonly used in the treatment of Cold Sputum, Sputum cough, and congested chest.

Contraindications: skin eruptions, eye disease, hemorrhoids, anal hemmorhage, and Hot diseases in general

Mutton

Nature:	Warm
Flavor:	Sweet
Meridian:	Spleen, Kidneys
Quality:	Yang
Elemental Quality:	Earth
Treatment Principles:	Tones Yang, tones Qi and Blood, benefits Qi, removes Blood Stagnation, expels Cold, sedates Yin, warms Middle Burner, warms Lower Burner

Commonly used in the treatment of indigestion, Deficiency fatigue, emaciation, cold sensations postpartum, sore loins, Cold abdominal pain, and Cold hernia.

Contraindications: Cold External diseases

Nori

Nature:	Cold
Flavor:	Sweet and Salty
Meridian:	Lungs
Direction:	Descending and Sinking
Quality:	Yin and Yang
Elemental Quality:	Earth
Treatment Principles:	Tonifies Qi and Blood, clears Heat, tones Yin, transforms Sputum, softens hardness, diuretic

Commonly used in the treatment of goiter, beriberi, edema, dysuria, cough, and hypertension.

Nutmeg

Nature:	Warm
Flavor:	Pungent
Meridian:	Large Intestine, Spleen
Direction:	Ascending
Quality:	Yang
Elemental Quality:	Metal
Treatment Principles:	Assists Yang, tones and regulates the Qi, benefits the Qi, removes Stagnant Blood, expels Cold, sedates Yin, warms the Middle Burner, lowers Rebellious Qi, promotes digestion, "solidifies" intestines

Commonly used in the treatment of abdominal pain and swelling, diarrhea, indigestion, and vomiting.

Octopus

Nature:	Cold
Flavor:	Sweet and Salty
Direction:	Descending
Quality:	Yin and Yang
Elemental Quality:	Earth
Treatment Principles:	Tonifies Qi and Blood, clears Heat, lubricates Dryness, tones Yin

Commonly used in the treatment of carbuncle.

Contraindications: urticaria

Olive

Nature:	Neutral
Flavor:	Sweet and Sour, Harsh
Meridian:	Lungs and Stomach
Direction:	Ascending and Descending
Quality:	Yin and Yang
Elemental Quality:	Wood and Earth
Treatment Principles:	Tonifies Qi and Blood, clears Lungs, benefits throat, produces Fluid, counteracts toxins

Commonly used in the treatment of sore throat, ulcers, thirst, cough, hemoptysis, epilepsy, alcoholism, and dysentery.

Onion

Nature:	Warm
Flavor:	Pungent
Direction:	Ascending
Quality:	Yang
Elemental Quality:	Earth
Treatment Principles:	Assists Yang, benefits and regulates Qi, tones the Qi, removes Blood Stagnation, expels Cold, sedates Yin, diaphoretic, counteracts toxins

Commonly used in the treatment of the common cold, headache, constipation, Cold abdominal pain, dysuria, dysentery, mastitis, nasal congestion, and facial edema.

Oyster

Nature:	Neutral
Flavor:	Sweet and Salty
Direction:	Ascending and Descending
Quality:	Yin and Yang
Elemental Quality:	Earth and Water
Treatment Principles:	Tones Qi and Blood, lubricates Dryness, tones Yin, nourishes the Blood

Commonly used in the treatment of insomnia, nervousness, erysipelas, and indecision.
Contraindications: leprosy and skin disease

Papaya

Nature:	Neutral
Flavor:	Sweet and Bitter, Harsh
Direction:	Ascending
Quality:	Yin and Yang
Elemental Quality:	Fire and Earth
Treatment Principles:	Tones Qi and Blood, dries Damp, promotes diaphoresis

Commonly used in the treatment of stomachache, dysentery, difficult bowel movements, difficult urination, and Wind Bi (rheumatism).

Peach

Nature:	Warm
Flavor:	Sweet and Sour
Direction:	Descending
Quality:	Yin and Yang
Elemental Quality:	Earth
Treatment Principles:	Assists Yang, tonifies Qi and Blood, benefits Qi, removes Blood Stagnation, expels Cold, produces Fluid, lubricates intestines, activates the Blood, eliminates accumulations

Commonly used in the treatment of Dry Lung cough, Hot Lung cough, and indigestion.

Overconsumption may create Internal Heat.

Peanut

Nature:	Neutral
Flavor:	Sweet
Meridian:	Lungs and Spleen
Direction:	Ascending
Quality:	Yang
Elemental Quality:	Earth
Treatment Principles:	Tonifies Qi and Blood, lubricates Lungs, harmonizes the Stomach

Commonly used in the treatment of Dry cough, indigestion, beriberi, agalactia, and chronic tracheitis.

Contraindications: Cold and/or Damp problems, Qi Stagnation, or diarrhea with discharge of sliding stools

Peanut Oil

Nature:	Neutral
Flavor:	Sweet
Direction:	Ascending
Quality:	Yang
Elemental Quality:	Earth
Treatment Principles:	Tonifies Qi and Blood, lubricates intestines, pushes accumulations downwards

Commonly used in the treatment of dysentery, intestinal obstruction caused by roundworms, acute conjunctivitis, and acute hepatitis.

Pear

Nature:	Cool
Flavor:	Sweet
Meridian:	Lungs and Stomach
Direction:	Descending
Quality:	Yin and Yang
Elemental Quality:	Wood and Earth
Treatment Principles:	Tonifies Qi and Blood, clears Heat, sedates Yang, produces Fluid, lubricates Dryness, transforms Sputum

Commonly used in the treatment of diabetes, Hot cough, dysphagia, and constipation.

Peas

Nature:	Neutral
Flavor:	Sweet
Meridian:	Stomach and Spleen
Direction:	Ascending
Quality:	Yang
Elemental Quality:	Earth
Treatment Principles:	Tones Qi and Blood, harmonizes Middle Burner, lowers Rebellious Qi, diuretic, induces bowel movements, counteracts skin eruptions

Commonly used for cholera, spasms, beriberi, and carbuncle.

Peppermint

Nature:	Cool
Flavor:	Pungent
Meridian:	Lungs and Liver
Direction:	Ascending
Quality:	Yin and Yang
Elemental Quality:	Metal
Treatment Principles:	Assists Yang, regulates Qi, tonifies the Blood, clears Heat, sedates Yang, benefits Qi, removes Blood Stagnation, disperses Wind, counteracts toxins

Commonly used in the treatment of External fever, headache, sore throat, indigestion, canker sore, toothache, skin eruptions, and migraine.

Contraindications: Liver Yang Ascension, Yin Deficiency, Blood Dryness or excessive perspiration '

Persimmon

Nature:	Cold
Flavor:	Sweet, Harsh
Meridian:	Lung, Large Intestine, Heart
Direction:	Descending
Quality:	Yin and Yang
Elemental Quality:	Earth
Treatment Principles:	Tonifies Qi and Blood, clears Heat, tones Yin, lubricates the Lungs, quenches thirst

Commonly used in the treatment of thirst, cough, hemoptysis, canker sore, and chronic bronchitis.

Contraindications: Stomach/Spleen Yang Deficiency, Damp Sputum, External cough, diarrhea, or malaria

Pineapple

Nature:	Neutral
Flavor:	Sweet
Direction:	Ascending
Quality:	Yang
Elemental Quality:	Earth
Treatment Principles:	Tonifies Qi and Blood, relieves Summer Heat, quenches thirst, promotes digestion, relieves diarrhea

Commonly used in treatment of oliguria, anorexia, edema, insomnia, thirst, and sunstroke.

Contraindications: Damp and/or Cold syndromes

Overconsumption may cause abdominal pain.

Pinenuts

Nature:	Warm
Flavor:	Sweet
Meridian:	Lung, Large Intestine, Liver
Quality:	Yang
Elemental Quality:	Earth
Treatment Principles:	Assists Yang, tones Qi and Blood, benefits Qi, removes Stagnant Blood, expels Cold, nourishes Fluids, expels Wind, lubricates Lungs, makes intestines "sliding"

Commonly used in treatment of Wind Bi (rheumatism), vertigo, Dry cough, hemoptysis, and constipation.

Plantain

Nature:	Cold
Flavor:	Sweet
Meridian:	Large and Small Intestine
Direction:	Descending
Quality:	Yin and Yang
Elemental Quality:	Earth
Treatment Principles:	Tones Qi and Blood, clears Heat, tones Yin, benefits Water, sharpens vision, expels Sputum

Commonly used in treatment of chronic tracheitis, anuria, dysuria, leukorrhea, hematuria, pertussis, jaundice, edema, dysentery, epistaxis, conjunctivitis, eye pain, and skin ulcers.

Contraindications: spermatorrhea (due to sliding nature of plantain)

Plum

Nature:	Neutral
Flavor:	Sweet and Sour
Meridian:	Kidneys and Liver
Direction:	Ascending and Descending
Quality:	Yin and Yang
Elemental Quality:	Wood and Earth
Treatment Principles:	Tonifies Qi and Blood, clears Liver, removes Heat, produces Fluid, benefits Water

Commonly used in the treatment of Deficiency fatigue, hot sensations, diabetes, ascites, and Liver disease.

Overconsumption may harm Stomach/Spleen in patients with Qi Deficiency.

Pork

Nature:	Neutral
Flavor:	Sweet and Salty
Meridian:	Stomach, Spleen, Kidneys
Direction:	Ascending and Descending
Quality:	Yin and Yang
Elemental Quality:	Earth and Water
Treatment Principles:	Tonifies Qi and Blood, lubricates Dryness, tones Yin

Commonly used in the treatment of diabetes, weakness, emaciation, Dry cough, and constipation.

Contraindications: Hot Damp Sputum or Qi Stagnation

Pork Kidney

Nature:	Neutral
Flavor:	Salty
Direction:	Descending
Quality:	Yin
Elemental Quality:	Water
Treatment Principles:	Lubricates Dryness, tones Kidneys, facilitates and benefits Bladder

Commonly used in the treatment of Kidney Deficiency lumbago, edema, spermatorrhea, night sweat, and senile deafness.

Potato

Nature:	Neutral
Flavor:	Sweet
Direction:	Ascending
Quality:	Yang
Elemental Quality:	Earth
Treatment Principles:	Tonifies Qi and Blood, tones the Spleen, heals inflammation

Commonly used in the treatment of mumps and burns.

Pumpkin

Nature:	Neutral
Flavor:	Sweet
Direction:	Ascending
Quality:	Yin and Yang
Elemental Quality:	Fire and Earth
Treatment Principles:	Tonifies Qi and Blood, dries Damp, induces diaphoresis

Commonly used in the treatment of bronchial asthma.

Radish

Nature:	Cool
Flavor:	Pungent and Sweet
Meridian:	Lungs, Stomach
Direction:	Ascending and Descending
Quality:	Yin and Yang
Elemental Quality:	Earth and Metal
Treatment Principles:	Assists Yang, regulates and tones the Qi, tones the Blood, clears Heat, sedates Yang, expels Cold, eliminates accumulations, transforms Sputum Heat (Glairy Mucous), lowers Rebellious Qi, expands the Middle Burner, counteracts toxins

Commonly used in the treatment of indigestion, abdominal swelling, Sputum cough, hoarseness, diabetes, occipital headache, hemoptysis, epistaxis, dysentery, and trichomonas vaginitis.

Contraindications: Deficiency Cold.

Raspberry

Nature:	Neutral
Flavor:	Sweet
Direction:	Ascending and Descending
Quality:	Yin and Yang
Elemental Quality:	Wood and Earth
Treatment Principles:	Tones Qi and Blood, tones Liver and Kidneys, checks urination, assists Yang, solidifies Jing, sharpens vision

Commonly used in the treatment of impotence, spermatorrhea, polyuria, enuresis, Deficiency fatigue, and blurred vision.

Contraindications: dysuria and priapism

Rice

Nature:	Neutral
Flavor:	Sweet
Meridian:	Stomach and Spleen
Direction:	Ascending
Quality:	Yang
Elemental Quality:	Earth
Treatment Principles:	Tonifies Qi and Blood, tones the Middle Burner, benefits the Qi, tones the Spleen, harmonizes the Stomach, relieves mental depression, quenches thirst, relieves diarrhea

Commonly used in the treatment of diarrhea, oliguria, and thirst.

Rice Bran

Nature:	Neutral
Flavor:	Pungent and Sweet
Meridian:	Large Intestine and Stomach
Direction:	Ascending
Quality:	Yang
Elemental Quality:	Earth and Metal
Treatment Principles:	Assists Yang, regulates Qi, tones Qi and Blood, reduces Fluids, removes Stagnant Blood, expels Cold, sedates Yin

Romaine Lettuce

Nature:	Cold
Flavor:	Bitter
Meridian:	Large Intestine and Stomach
Quality:	Yin
Elemental Quality:	Fire
Treatment Principles:	Tonifies Qi and Blood, clears Heat, sedates Yang, dries Dampness, promotes diuresis

Commonly used in the treatment of alcoholism.

Rosemary

Nature:	Warm
Flavor:	Pungent
Direction:	Ascending
Quality:	Yang
Elemental Quality:	Metal
Treatment Principles:	Assists Yang, benefits and regulates Qi, removes Stagnant Blood, expels Cold, sedates Yin, strengthens the Stomach, diaphoretic, calms Spirit

Commonly used in the treatment of headache and prevention of premature baldness.

Slightly toxic

Rye

Nature:	Neutral
Flavor:	Bitter
Direction:	Ascending
Quality:	Yin
Elemental Quality:	Fire
Treatment Principles:	Dries Damp, diuretic

Commonly used in the treatment of postpartum hemorrhage and migraine.

Considered toxic

Safflower

Nature:	Warm
Flavor:	Pungent
Meridian:	Heart and Liver
Direction:	Ascending
Quality:	Yang
Elemental Quality:	Metal
Treatment Principles:	Assists Yang; tones, regulates, and benefits Qi, expels Cold, removes Blood Stagnation, activates Blood, eumenogogue, analgesic

Commonly used in the treatment of bed sores, amenorrhea, abdominal swelling and obstruction, difficult labor, stillbirth, carbuncle, postpartum suppression of lochia, and coronary heart disease.

Contraindications: pregnancy

Saffron

Nature:	Neutral
Flavor:	Sweet and Sour
Meridian:	Heart and Liver
Direction:	Ascending and Descending
Quality:	Yin and Yang
Elemental Quality:	Wood and Earth
Treatment Principles:	Tonifies Qi and Blood, activates the Blood, transforms coagulations, disperses Stagnant Qi

Commonly used in the treatment of chest congestion, hemoptysis, amenorrhea, postpartum abdominal pain, and contusions.

Contraindications: pregnancy

Salt

Nature:	Cold
Flavor:	Salty
Meridian:	Large Intestine, Stomach, Small Intestine, Kidneys
Direction:	Sinking
Quality:	Yin
Elemental Quality:	Water
Treatment Principles:	Clears Heat, lubricates Dryness, tones Yin, induces vomiting, cools the Blood, counteracts toxins

Commonly used in the treatment of abdominal swelling and pain, difficult bowel movements, dysuria, pyorrhea, sore throat, toothache, corneal opacity, and skin eruptions.

Contraindications: edema

Sardine

Nature:	Neutral
Flavor:	Sweet and Salty
Meridian:	Stomach and Spleen
Direction:	Ascending and Descending
Quality:	Yin and Yang
Elemental Quality:	Earth and Water
Treatment Principles:	Tonifies Qi and Blood, lubricates Dryness, tones Yin, warms the Middle Burner, benefits the Qi, strengthens tendons and bones, activates the Blood, diuretic, digestant

Commonly used in the treatment of urinary strain.

Overconsumption may cause Fire and Sputum.

Scallion

Nature:	Warm
Flavor:	Pungent and Bitter
Meridian:	Lungs, Large Intestine, Heart
Direction:	Ascending
Quality:	Yin and Yang
Elemental Quality:	Fire and Metal
Treatment Principles:	Assists Yang, tones, regulates and benefits the Qi, clears Heat, sedates Yang, dries Damp, diuretic, removes Blood Stagnation, expels Cold, expands the chest, disperses coagulations

Commonly used in the treatment of chest pain, heart pain, dry retching, diarrhea, and skin eruptions.

Contraindications: Qi Deficiency

Seaweed

Nature:	Cold
Flavor:	Salty
Direction:	Sinking
Quality:	Yin
Elemental Quality:	Water
Treatment Principles:	Clears Heat, lubricates Dryness, tones Yin, softens hardness, transforms Sputum, benefits Water

Commonly used in the treatment of goiter, abdominal swelling and obstruction, edema, and beriberi.

Sesame Oil

Nature:	Cool
Flavor:	Sweet
Meridian:	Stomach
Direction:	Descending
Quality:	Yin and Yang
Elemental Quality:	Earth
Treatment Principles:	Tonifies Qi and Blood, clears Heat, sedates Yang, lubricates Dryness, induces bowel movements, counteracts toxins, ''produces muscles''

Commonly used in the treatment of dry stool constipation, abdominal pain due to indigestion, roundworms, skin eruptions, ulcer, scabies, and dry skin.

Contraindications: Spleen Deficiency diarrhea

Shark Meat

Nature:	Neutral
Flavor:	Sweet and Salty
Meridian:	Spleen
Direction:	Ascending and Descending
Quality:	Yin and Yang
Elemental Quality:	Earth and Water
Treatment Principles:	Tonifies Qi and Blood, lubricates Dryness, tones Yin, tonifies the Five Viscera, heals swellings, removes coagulations

Shepherd's Purse

Nature:	Neutral
Flavor:	Sweet
Meridian:	Liver
Direction:	Ascending
Quality:	Yang
Elemental Quality:	Earth
Treatment Principles:	Tonifies Qi and Blood, harmonizes the Spleen, benefits Water, arrests bleeding, sharpens vision

Commonly used in the treatment of diarrhea, edema, dysuria, chyluria, hemoptysis, hemafecia, vaginal bleeding, menorrhagia, conjunctivitis, prevention of measles, and postpartum hemorrhage.

Shiitake Mushroom

Nature:	Neutral
Flavor:	Sweet
Meridian:	Stomach
Direction:	Ascending
Quality:	Yang
Elemental Quality:	Earth
Treatment Principles:	Tonifies Qi and Blood, benefits the Stomach

Commonly used in treatment of hunger.
Contraindicated during convalescence of chicken pox, childbirth or general illness.

Shrimp

Nature:	Warm
Flavor:	Sweet
Quality:	Yang
Elemental Quality:	Earth
Treatment Principles:	Assists and tonifies the Yang, tones Qi and Blood, benefits Qi, removes Blood Stagnation, expels Cold, eliminates Wind, expels Sputum, destroys worms, promotes lactation

Contraindications: Hot Blood skin disorders and while recuperating from chronic illness

Sorghum

Nature:	Warm
Flavor:	Sweet
Meridian:	Lungs, Large Intestine, Stomach, Spleen
Quality:	Yang
Elemental Quality:	Earth
Treatment Principles:	Assists Yang, tonifies Qi and Blood, benefits Qi, removes Stagnant Blood, expels Cold, warms the Middle Burner, constricts the Stomach and Intestines

Commonly used in the treatment of pediatric indigestion, rheumatism, oliguria, and diarrhea.

Soybean

Nature:	Cool
Flavor:	Sweet
Meridian:	Large Intestine and Spleen
Direction:	Descending
Quality:	Yin and Yang
Elemental Quality:	Earth
Treatment Principles:	Tonifies Qi and Blood, clears Heat, sedates Yang, strengthens Spleen, expands Middle Burner, lubricates Dryness, eliminates water

Commonly used in the treatment of malnutrition in children, diarrhea, abdominal swelling, emaciation, skin eruptions, and hemorrhage from trauma.

Overconsumption may cause Qi Stagnation, Sputum, cough, yellowish complexion, and/or heavy sensations in the body.

Soybean Oil

Nature:	Hot
Flavor:	Pungent and Sweet
Direction:	Ascending and Floating
Quality:	Yang
Elemental Quality:	Earth and Metal
Treatment Principles:	Assists Yang, tonifies and regulates the Qi, tonifies the Blood, benefits the Qi, removes Blood Stagnation, expels Cold, sedates Yin, expels worms, lubricates the intestines

Commonly used in the treatment of constipation and intestinal obstruction.

Slightly toxic

Spearmint

Nature:	Warm
Flavor:	Pungent and Sweet
Direction:	Ascending
Quality:	Yang
Elemental Quality:	Earth and Metal
Treatment Principles:	Assists Yang, tonifies Qi and Blood, benefits Qi, removes Stagnant Blood, expels Cold, sedates Yin, disperses Wind, analgesic, regulates Qi

Commonly used in the treatment of the common cold, cough, headache, dysmenorrhea, and abdominal pain.

Spinach

Nature:	Cool
Flavor:	Sweet
Meridian:	Large and Small Intestine
Direction:	Descending
Quality:	Yin and Yang
Elemental Quality:	Earth
Treatment Principles:	Tonifies Qi and Blood, clears Heat, sedates Yang, nourishes the Blood, hemostatic, constricts Yin, lubricates Dryness

Commonly used in the treatment of epistaxis, hemafecia, scurvy, diabetes, thirst, and difficult bowel movements.

Contraindications: spermatorrhea

Squash

Nature:	Warm
Flavor:	Sweet
Meridian:	Stomach and Spleen
Quality:	Yang
Elemental Quality:	Earth
Treatment Principles:	Assists Yang, tonifies Qi and Blood, benefits Qi, removes Stagnant Blood, expels Cold, sedates Yin, tonifies the Middle Burner, heals inflammation, analgesic

Contraindications: Qi Stagnation and/or Damp Obstruction.

Strawberry

Nature:	Warm
Flavor:	Sweet and Sour
Direction:	Descending
Quality:	Yin and Yang
Elemental Quality:	Wood and Earth
Treatment Principles:	Assists Yang, tonifies Qi and Blood, benefits Qi, removes Stagnant Blood, expels Cold, tones the Liver and Kidneys, checks urination

Commonly used in the treatment of polyuria, vertigo, and motion sickness.

String Bean

Nature:	Neutral
Flavor:	Sweet
Meridian:	Spleen and Kidneys
Quality:	Yang
Elemental Quality:	Earth
Treatment Principles:	Tonifies Qi and Blood, tones Yin, strengthens Spleen, tonifies Kidneys

Commonly used in the treatment of polyuria, diarrhea, emesis, diabetes, spermatorrhea (with erotic dreams), and leukorrhea.

Contraindications: Qi Stagnation and constipation.

Sturgeon

Nature:	Neutral
Flavor:	Sweet
Meridian:	Lungs, Pericardium
Direction:	Ascending
Quality:	Yang
Elemental Quality:	Earth
Treatment Principles:	Tonifies Qi and Blood, benefits Qi, activates Blood, relieves urinary strains, nutritive

Commonly used in the treatment of hematuria.

Sugar (refined)

Nature:	Neutral
Flavor:	Sweet
Meridian:	Spleen
Direction:	Ascending
Quality:	Yang
Elemental Quality:	Earth
Treatment Principles:	Tones Qi and Blood, lubricates Lungs, produces Fluid

Commonly used in the treatment of Dry cough, thirst, and stomachache.

Contraindications: Damp Sputum

Sweet Potato

Nature:	Warm
Flavor:	Neutral and Sweet
Meridian:	Spleen and Kidneys
Direction:	Ascending
Quality:	Yang
Elemental Quality:	Earth
Treatment Principles:	Assists Yang, tonifies Qi and Blood, benefits Qi, removes Stagnant Blood, expels Cold, tonifies the Middle Burner, harmonizes the Blood, produces Fluid, expands the Stomach and Intestines, induces bowel movements, and makes the Five Viscera "fat"

Commonly used in the treatment of diarrhea, jaundice, emaciation and skin eruption.

Contraindications: Middle Burner congestion and Qi Congestion.

Sweet Rice (glutinous rice)

Nature:	Warm
Flavor:	Sweet
Meridian:	Lungs
Quality:	Yang
Elemental Quality:	Earth
Treatment Principles:	Assists Yang, tonifies Qi and Blood, benefits Qi, removes Stagnant Blood, expels Cold, sedates Yin, tones the Middle Burner

Commonly used in the treatment of diabetes, polyuria, excessive perspiration, and diarrhea.

Contraindications: Stomach/Spleen Yang Deficiency, Sputum Heat or Wind disease

Swiss Chard

Nature:	Cool
Flavor:	Sweet
Meridian:	Lungs, Large Intestine, Stomach, Spleen
Direction:	Descending
Quality:	Yin and Yang
Elemental Quality:	Earth
Treatment Principles:	Tonifies Qi and Blood, clears Heat, sedates Yang, counteracts toxins, relieves coagulations, hemostatic

Commonly used in the treatment of delayed eruption of measles, dysentery, amenorrhea, and carbuncle.

Tangerine

Nature:	Cool
Flavor:	Sweet and Sour
Meridian:	Lungs, Stomach, Spleen
Direction:	Descending
Quality:	Yin and Yang
Elemental Quality:	Wood and Earth
Treatment Principles:	Tonifies Qi and Blood, clears Heat, sedates Yang, appetant, regulates Qi, quenches thirst, lubricates Lungs

Commonly used in the treatment of chest congestion, vomiting, diabetes and hiccough.

Contraindications: cough and sputum from Wind Cold attack

Taro

Nature:	Neutral
Flavor:	Pungent and Sweet
Meridian:	Large Intestine, Stomach
Direction:	Ascending
Quality:	Yang
Elemental Quality:	Earth and Metal
Treatment Principles:	Assists Yang, tones and regulates Qi, tones the Blood, benefits Qi, removes Blood Stagnation, disperses coagulations

Commonly used in the treatment of scrofula, swelling, abdominal lump, psoriasis, and burns.

Fresh taro considered toxic.

Tofu

Nature:	Cool
Flavor:	Sweet
Meridian:	Lungs, Large Intestine, Stomach
Direction:	Descending
Quality:	Yin and Yang
Elemental Quality:	Earth
Treatment Principles:	Tonifies Qi and Blood, clears Heat, sedates Yang, tones Yin, harmonizes the Middle Burner, produces Fluid, lubricates Dryness, counteracts toxins

Commonly used in the treatment of conjunctivitis, chronic amoebic dysentery, diabetes, sulfur poisoning, and alcoholism.

Contraindications: spermatorrhea

Tomato

Nature:	Cold
Flavor:	Sweet and Sour
Direction:	Descending
Quality:	Yin and Yang
Elemental Quality:	Wood and Earth
Treatment Principles:	Tonifies Qi and Blood, clears Heat, tones Yin, produces Fluid, quenches thirst, strengthens Stomach, promotes digestion

Commonly used in the treatment of thirst and anorexia.

Trout

Nature:	Hot
Flavor:	Sour
Quality:	Yin and Yang
Elemental Quality:	Wood
Treatment Principles:	Assists Yang, regulates Qi, expels Cold, sedates Yin, warms Stomach, harmonizes the Middle Burner

Overconsumption will generate Wind and Heat and cause skin eruptions and scabies.

Turnip

Nature:	Neutral
Flavor:	Pungent, Sweet, Bitter
Direction:	Ascending
Quality:	Yin and Yang
Elemental Quality:	Fire, Earth, Metal
Treatment Principles:	Assists Yang, tones, regulates and benefits Qi, tones Blood, removes Blood Stagnation, clears Heat, sedates Yang, dries Damp, diaphoretic, expels Cold, sedates Yin, appetant, lowers Rebellious Qi, counteracts toxins

Commonly used in the treatment of indigestion, jaundice, diabetes, swelling, and mastitis.

Overconsumption may cause swelling.

Vinegar

Nature:	Warm
Flavor:	Sour and Bitter
Meridian:	Stomach and Liver
Direction:	Descending
Quality:	Yin and Yang
Elemental Quality:	Wood and Fire
Treatment Principles:	Assists Yang, tonifies Qi, dries Damp, induces perspiration, benefits Qi, removes Stagnant Blood, expels Cold, sedates Yin, disperses coagulations, hemostatic, counteracts toxins, vermifuge

Commonly used in the treatment of postpartum syncope, abdominal swelling and obstruction, jaundice, hemoptysis, epistaxis, hemafecia, general pruritis, carbuncle, and food poisoning.

Contraindications: Stomach/Spleen Yang Deficiency, muscular atrophy, rheumatism, tendon trauma, onset of the common cold

Walnut

Nature:	Warm
Flavor:	Sweet
Meridian:	Lungs and Kidneys
Quality:	Yang
Elemental Quality:	Earth
Treatment Principles:	Tones Qi and Blood, benefits Qi, removes Blood Stagnation, expels Cold, sedates Yin, tonifies Kidneys, solidifies sperm, warms Lungs, calms asthma, lubricates intestines

Commonly used in the treatment of asthma, cough, lumbago, impotence, spermatorrhea, polyuria, urinary lithiasis, and dry stools.

Contraindications: Sputum Fire or Yin Deficiency with False Fire Flaring

Water Chestnut

Nature:	Cold
Flavor:	Sweet
Meridian:	Lungs and Stomach
Direction:	Descending
Quality:	Yin
Elemental Quality:	Earth
Treatment Principles:	Clears Heat, tones Yin, transforms Sputum, disperses accumulations

Commonly used in the treatment of diabetes, jaundice, conjunctivitis, measles, dysentery with bloody stools, and smoker's sore throat.

Contraindications: Deficiency, Cold or Blood Deficiency syndromes

Watercress

Nature:	Cool
Flavor:	Pungent and Sweet
Meridian:	Lungs and Stomach
Direction:	Ascending and Descending
Quality:	Yin and Yang
Elemental Quality:	Earth and Metal
Treatment Principles:	Assists Yang, regulates, benefits and tones Qi, tones Blood, removes Blood Stagnation, expels Cold, clears Heat, sedates Yang, benefits Water

Commonly used in the treatment of jaundice, edema, urinary strain, leukorrhea, scrofula, mumps, and oliguria.

Contraindications: Stomach/Spleen Deficiency, Cold Middle Burner or polyuria

Watermelon

Nature:	Cold
Flavor:	Sweet
Meridian:	Stomach, Heart, Bladder
Direction:	Descending
Quality:	Yin and Yang
Elemental Quality:	Earth
Treatment Principles:	Tonifies Qi and Blood, clears Heat, tones Yin, relieves Summer Heat, relieves mental depression, quenches thirst, diuretic

Commonly used in the treatment of thirst, oliguria, sore throat, and canker sores.

Contraindications: Cold Middle Burner, Excess Damp, anemia or polyuria

Wheat

Nature:	Cool
Flavor:	Sweet
Meridian:	Spleen, Heart, Kidneys
Direction:	Descending
Quality:	Yin and Yang
Elemental Quality:	Earth
Treatment Principles:	Tonifies Qi and Blood, clears Heat, sedates Yang, nourishes Heart, calms the Spirit, tones the Kidneys, quenches thirst

Wheat Bran

Nature:	Cool
Flavor:	Sweet
Meridian:	Large Intestine
Direction:	Descending
Quality:	Yin and Yang
Elemental Quality:	Earth
Treatment Principles:	Tonifies Qi and Blood, clears Heat, sedates Yang

Wheat Germ

Nature:	Cold
Flavor:	Pungent
Meridian:	Heart and Small Intestine
Direction:	Ascending
Quality:	Yin and Yang
Elemental Quality:	Metal
Treatment Principles:	Assists Yang, regulates Qi, clears Heat, tones Yin, benefits Qi, removes Stagnant Blood, relieves mental depression

Commonly used in the treatment of alcoholism.

Whitefish

Nature:	Neutral
Flavor:	Sweet
Meridian:	Lungs, Stomach, Liver
Direction:	Ascending
Quality:	Yang
Elemental Quality:	Earth
Treatment Principles:	Tonifies Qi and Blood, appetant, tones Spleen, relieves indigestion, promotes flow of Water

White Fungus

Nature:	Neutral
Flavor:	Sweet and Neutral
Quality:	Yang
Elemental Quality:	Earth
Treatment Principles:	Tonifies Qi and Blood, eliminates Damp, diuretic, waters Yin, lubricates Lungs, nourishes Stomach, produces Fluid

Commonly used in the treatment of cough with blood-specked sputum and thirst.

Contraindications: spermatorrhea

White Pepper

Nature:	Cold
Flavor:	Pungent and Bitter
Direction:	Ascending
Quality:	Yin and Yang
Elemental Quality:	Fire and Metal
Treatment Principles:	Assists Yang, clears Heat, sedates Yang, dries Damp, diaphoretic, tones Yin, benefits Qi, removes Stagnant Blood, analgesic, expels Wind

Commonly used in the treatment of the common cold, cough, sore throat, toothache, stomachache, rheumatic arthritis, dysentery and elephantiasis of the lower limbs.

Yam

Nature:	Neutral
Flavor:	Sweet
Meridian:	Lungs, Spleen, Kidneys
Direction:	Ascending
Quality:	Yang
Elemental Quality:	Earth
Treatment Principles:	Tonifies Qi and Blood, tones Spleen, tones Lungs, solidifies Kidneys, benefits semen

Commonly used in the treatment of diarrhea, dysentery, cough, diabetes, spermatorrhea, leukorrhea, polyuria, and acute bacillary dysentery.

Contraindications: Excess diseases

Footnotes

[1] Chuang Tsu, **Chuang Tsu: Inner Chapters**, trans. G.F. Feng & J. English (New York: Vintage Books, 1974), p. 55.

[2] The Eight Limbs of Classical Chinese Medicine are a way of schematizing oriental science in relation to health and healing. Such a schema emphasizes the cosmological aspect of health and the holistic treatment of disease. It also defines the hierarchy of the therapeutic modes. The Eight Limbs are comprised of Meditation, Exercise, Diet, Astrology, Geomancy, Massage, Herbology, and Acupuncture /Moxibustion. This conceptual approach is classical in so far as its principles and methodology are based on all the major classics of Chinese medicine stretching from the *Nei Jing* up through the Ching dynasty and to today. As such, it should be seen in contradistinction to what is being promulgated under the title "Traditional Acupuncture," an incomplete style of acupuncture created in England without reference to the primary literature of Chinese medicine, and to the current trend in the Peoples' Republic of China where Traditional Chinese Medicine is a watered-down version of classical practice liberally admixed with western scientific revisions. The creation of the Eight Limbs schema has been influenced by the eight divisions of both Indian Ayurvedic medicine and Tibetan Buddhist medicine. It has also been influenced by Professor Chee Soo's description of the "Eight Strands of Brocade" in Chee Soo, **The Tao of Long Life** (New York: Sterling Publications, 1984).

[3] In fact, it should be said that peoples' diets in China and other Asian countries today are not necessarily more healthful than modern American fare. The average Chinese does not eat consciously according to Chinese medical theory. Therefore, as Americans, we should be careful to avoid the assumption that since the Chinese (or Japanese or Koreans, etc.) eat something we should too, as in, for instance, the use of MSG.

191

[4] Those interested in reading further about *Chu-len* are referred to the translation of a Tibetan *Chu-len* text written by the Second Dalai Lama in the early sixteenth century: Library of Tibetan Works and Archives, "Extracting the Essence," *Tibetan Medicine*, Series No. 5 (Dharamsala, India: Library of Tibetan Works and Archives, 1982). This text deals with a system of *Me-tok Chu-len* or "Flower Alchemy" in which the practitioner ingests flower petals instead of inorganic substances as their sole form of physical food. The reader should note that this practice involves religious ritual, consecration, and disciplines. Also the reader should note the very clear instructions to the Guru in selecting a student who is a worthy candidate for such a practice.

[5] Some western readers may not believe that such a physical apotheosis is possible. Any evidence that I could put forward is no more than hearsay since I have never seen such an event myself. Over the past fifteen years, I have heard from a number of Tibetan Lamas of specific yogis in specific villages or areas achieving the Rainbow Body on specific dates. I also have in my possession a color photograph of the late H.H. Karmapa Rinpoche, former hierarch of the Karma Kagyud order, demonstrating his Rainbow Body two years before his death in 1981. Copies of this photo are available from Kagyu Droden Kunchap 1892 Fell St., San Francisco, CA 94117.

[6] Pang, T.Y., **Chinese Herbal: An Introduction** (Honolulu, HI: Tai Chi School of Philosophy and Art, 1982), p. 44.

[7] A simple but accurate description of Triple Heater energetics is given in Henry Woolerton and E. McLean, **Acupuncture Energy In Health and Disease** (Wellingborough, England: Thorsons Publishers, 1979).

[8] The terms Little Fire and Big Fire are based on their usage as introduced in Kiiko Matsumoto and Stephen Birch, **Five Elements and Ten Stems** (Brookline, MA: Paradigm Publications, 1983), p. 69.

[9] **Nei Jing Su Wen**, Chapter 23.

[10] **Nei Jing Ling Shu**, Chapter 78.

[11] Unspecified classic, presumed to be the **Nei Jing**; quoted by Pang, *op.cit.*, p. 44.

[12] Based on Phase Energetics, described in English in Manfred Porkert, **Theoretical Foundations of Chinese Medicine** (Cambridge: MIT

Press, 1977); and in Chinese in Chang Ching Yue, **Lei Ching T'u I**, through prognosis of meterological changes in the Six Qi (Wind, Hot, Cold, Dry, Damp, and Fire) one might be able to eat more or less of one of the six flavors in order to adjust for unseasonable or severe climatic effects on the internal energetic environment. However, Phase Energetics, formerly believed by many classical physicians to be the pinnacle of Chinese cosmological medicine, is viewed by many contemporary practitioners both in Asia and the West as being too simplistic to be an adequate forecasting tool. And, although I personally do place great store in the prognosticative abilities of Phase Energetics within certain limitations, it is too complex a procedure for either the average patient or practitioner to make frequent use. Therefore preventive use of the six flavors based on Phase Energetics has not been included in this work.

[13] **Nei Jing**, quoted by Pang, *op.cit.*, p. 47.

[14] The reader should be warned that the definition of Yin and Yang according to classical Chinese medicine is at variance with the definition used in Macrobiotics. According to Chinese medicine Yang is active, expansive, extraversive, centrifugal, aggressive, demanding, and negative. Yin is structive, contractive, absorbent, internalizing, centripetal, responsive, conservative, and positive. These definitions are based on the erudite scholarship of Manfred Porkert, **Theoretical Foundations of Chinese Medicine**, *op.cit.*. All mention and use of the concepts Yin and Yang in this book are made from the Chinese point of view as substantiated by the classics and not from the Macrobiotic point of view, a contemporary Japanese school of dietary therapy whose proponents never cite the source(s) of their own, idiosyncratic definitions.

[15] S. Dharmananda, "Chinese Herbal Therapy for Multiple Allergies," *Oriental Healing Arts Newsletter*, Vol. 1, No. 2, Summer 1983: 1-2.

[16] Hsu, H.Y., **For Women Only: Chinese Herbal Formulas** (Long Beach, CA: Oriental Healing Arts Institute, 1982), p. 8.

[17] **Alchemy, Medicine, and Religion in the China of A.D. 320: The Nei P'ien of Ko Hung**, Ware, J.R., trans. (Cambridge: MIT Press, 1966), pp. 113-114.

[18] Shanghai College of Traditional Chinese Medicine, **Essentials of Chinese Acupuncture** (Beijing: Foreign Language Press, 1980), p. 46.

[19] Chang Chung-Ching, **Chin Kuei Yao Lueh** ⟨ Prescriptions from the Golden Chamber ⟩, Hong-yen Hsu and Chau-Shin Hsu, trans. Long Beach, CA: (Oriental Healing Arts Institute, 1983), p. 171.

[20] *Mahavagga*, Horner, I.B., trans., **Book of the Discipline** ⟨ *Vinaya-pitaka* ⟩, vol. IV (London: *Mahavagga*, 1951), p. 302.

[21] Li Shih-Zhen, *Chinese Medicinal Herbs*, F.P. Smith and G.A. Stuart, trans. (San Francisco: Georgetown Press, 1973), pp. 471-474. This book purports to be based on Li Shih Chen's *Pen Tsao Kang Mu* but it is not a literal translation of that famous classic.

[22] Chang Chung-Ching, **Shang Han Lun** ⟨ Treatise on Febrile Diseases ⟩, H. Y. Hsu and W. G. Preacher, trans. (Los Angeles: Oriental Healing Arts, 1981), p. 167.

[23] F.W. Zhou, "The Indications of Decoction Ramulus Cinnamomi Composite," C. S. Cheung and M. Hirano, trans., *Journal of the American College of Traditional Chinese Medicine* 1 (San Francisco: American College of Traditional Chinese Medicine, 1983), p. 11.

[24] Lilah Kan, **Introducing Chinese Casserole Cookery** (New York: Workman Publishing, 1978), pp. 11 and 12.

[25] T. Y. Pang, *op.cit.*, p. 70.

Bibliography

Pang, T.Y. **Chinese Herbal, An Introduction**. Honolulu: Tai Chi School of Philosophy and Art, 1982.

Zhen, Li-Shih. **Chinese Medicinal Herbs**. Translated by F. Porter Smith and G. A. Stuart. San Francisco: Georgetown Press, 1973.

Chinese Herb Medicine & Therapy. Translated by Hong-yen Hsu and William G. Peacher. Los Angeles: Oriental Healing Arts Institute of U.S.A., 1976.

Lu, Henry C. **Doctor's Manual of Chinese Medical Diet**. Vancouver, BC: Academy of Oriental Heritage, 1981.

Da Liu. **The Tao of Health and Longevity**. New York: Schocken Books, 1979.

Soo, Chee. **The Tao of Long Life**. New York: Sterling Publications, 1984.

Porkert, Manfred. **Theoretical Foundations of Chinese Medicine**. Cambridge: MIT Press, 1982.

Kaptchuk, Ted J. **The Web That Has No Weaver**. New York: Congdon and Weed, 1983.

Chinese Cookbooks for Further Recipes

Chinese Health Foods. Tokyo: Shinfunomoto Company, 1972.

Fessler, Stella Lau. **Chinese Meatless Cooking**. New York: New American Library, 1980.

Kan, Lilah. **Introducing Chinese Casserole Cookery**. New York: Workman Publishing, 1978.

Gain, Margaret and Castle, Alfred E. **Regional Cooking of China**. San Francisco: 101 Productions, 1975.

Chinese Sources on Dietetics

Jen, Ch'en Ts'un, ed. **Er Ch'ang Shih Wu Yang Sheng Fa** ⟨ The Method of Nurturing Life by Daily Food ⟩.

Ching, Wu Chia, ed., with Ts'un Jen, research associate. **Yang Sheng Pao Chien Shih P'u** ⟨ Handbook of Nurturing Life and Preserving Health by Food ⟩.

Ch'uan, Chou Ch'ien, ed. **Ch'i Kung Yao Ni Liao Fa Yuan Li** ⟨ Fundamental Principles of Therapeutics Through Ch'i Kung and Herbal Medications ⟩.

Hsien, Meng. **Shih Liao Pen Ts'ao** ⟨ Compendium of Dietetic Therapeutics ⟩.

Many thanks to Paul Gallagher of the Deer Mountain Taoist Academy, R.D. 3, Box 109A, Guilford, VT 05301.

General Index

Abdominal distention, 39, 42, 45, 46
abdominal surgery, 52
abortions, 52
aches, 59
acid eructation, 46
adolescents, 13
aduki bean, 42
agar, 41, 42, 60
alcohol, 43, 44, 47, 63, 67
alfalfa, 42
allergic rhinitis, 35, 43
allergies, 57
almond, 60
amasake, 35, 36, 47, 53, 68
amenorrhea, 51, 52, 73
anchovy, 36, 41, 42
anemia, 39, 51
anger, 46
animal kidney, 52
animal protein, 58
anorexia, 41
anxiety, 43, 51
appetite excessive but loosing weight, 45
apple, 36, 55, 60, 61, 64
arrowroot, 41
arthralgia, 43
arthritis, 64
Ascension of Liver Yang, 48
asparagus, 36, 60, 64
asthma, 58
Astragalus, 57, 61
Bamboo shoot, 42
banana, 35, 64
barley, 42, 64
barley malt, 41, 61, 62
basil, 47, 53
bay leaf, 36, 47
beef, 41, 47
beer, 44
beet, 47, 65
belching, 42
belladonna, 73
Bi syndrome, 64
bitter taste, 19
black fungus, 51, 68
black pepper, 36, 41, 47
black poultices, 77

black sesame, 42, 47, 65
black soybean, 65
Blood Deficiency, 51, 68
Blood Energy, 51
Blood or Yin Deficiency, 54
Blood Stagnation, 32
boils, 8
bones, weak, 71
bowel movements, 32, 54
breakthrough menstrual bleeding, 32
bronchitis, 58, 62
broth, 57, 59, 61, 64, 71
Cayenne, 41
celery, 36, 47, 48, 50, 51, 60, 62, 64
cellulite, 65
cephalgia, 48
cervical cancer, 53
cervical dysplasia, 31
chapped lips, 52
cheese, 41, 55, 68
cherry, 36, 37, 41
chestnut, 35, 42, 53, 64, 68
chicken, 35, 41, 42, 47, 52
chills, 59
Chinese dates, 51
chocolate, 43, 67
chronic amenorrhea, 52
cinnamon, 41
circulation, problems of, 8
citrus fruit, 35, 41, 44
clam, 42, 55, 61
clinical depression, 46
cocks-crow diarrhea, 64
coconut milk, 35, 36, 37, 42, 47, 60, 68
coffee, 44, 47, 67
cold hands and feet, 39, 57
Cold Obstruction, 32
Cold syndrome, 28
Cold Wasting, 45
colds and flu, frequent, 43
colitis, 39
colonics, 55, 9
conjunctivitis, 48
consciousness, 62
constipation, 48, 52, 54
constipation from Blood or Yin, 54

food, temperature of, 18, 19, 8
food to promote diaphoresis, 36
food, Warm, 19, 35
food, Yin/Yang balance, 18, 21
foods, excessively salty, 58
foods, excessively sweet, 58
foods for Spleen Qi Deficiency, 41
foods for Spleen Yang Deficiency, 41
foods, heavy, 20
foods, Kidney tonifying, 44
foods, light, 20
foods, Warm, 10, 20
foods with ascending nature, 36
foods, Yang flavored, 20
foods, Yin flavored, 20
Four Directions, 20
Four Natures, 19
Four Phases, 7, 13
frustration, 46
fullness of chest, 41
furuncles, 66
Gan Qi, 46
garlic, 35, 42, 47, 60, 62
gastric ulcers, 39
gastritis, 39
gastroenteritis, chronic, 41
generalized tension, 43
Gerson diet, 2, 57, 65
ginger, 41, 47, 57, 60, 62, 65
Heart function, suppresssed, 71
heartburn, 46
Heat in the Blood, 68
Heaven, Man, and Earth, 7, 11
Heavenly Retribution diseases, 47, 66
hemorrhoids, 8
hepatitis, 39, 41
herbs, 2, 18, 55, 64, 78
Herpes genitalia, 32, 66
hiccough, 42
high blood pressure, 38, 48
hives, 43
homeopathy, 19
homeostasis, 11
honey, 41, 55, 60, 62
Hot Blood, 30
Hot Lungs, 58, 60, 61
Hot Wasting, 45
Huang Qi, 57
Humoral syndromes, 18
hyperactivity, 63, 70
hypertension, 48, 8
Impatience, 43
impotence, 45, 64

Infants, 13
influenza, 57, 58, 62
insomnia, 48, 63
Internal disease, 36
irritability, 46, 48, 63
Jing, 11, 32, 62, 51, 55
Jing, Qi, and Shen, 11
Job's tears, 42, 60, 62, 65
joints, puffy and swollen, 65
Jue Yin level of disease, 62
Kelly diet, 77
kelp, 42, 47, 50
kholrabi, 47
kidney, 35
kidney bean, 42, 68
Kidney Deficiency, 44, 67, 81, 9
Kidney Fire, 13, 14, 43, 62
Kidney, in blood formation, 51
Kidney Water, 62
Kidney weakness, 9
Kidney Yang, 37, 43
Kidney Yin, 37, 62, 63
Kidneys, 10, 20, 32, 56, 64, 67, 68
kohlrabi, 42, 60, 62
kudzu, 42
kudzu root, 41
Laetrile, 77
large appetite, 43
leek, 35, 36, 37, 41, 47, 57
lettuce, 48, 64
leukorrhea, 39, 41
litchi, 35, 36, 37, 41, 47
Liver, 20, 26, 42, 56, 68
Liver extract pills, 81
Liver Fire Blazing Upward, 26, 28, 48
Liver Invading Spleen, 26
Liver Qi, 31, 46, 54, 68
Liver relaxing foods, 47
Liver Yang Excess, 48, 49
Liver Yang Rising, 43
Liver Yang, sedation of, 48
Liver Yin, tonification of, 48
loneliness, 43
longan, 47, 64, 68
longevity, 17, 7
loose stools, 39
loss of memory, 63
lotus root, 68
lotus seed, for premature ejaculation, 64
low back pain, 45, 51, 52, 63
low back tension, 43
low back weaknesss, 63
Lower Burner, 55, 56, 67, 68

premature ejaculation, 63, 64
premenstrual discomfort, 31
premenstrual syndrome, 46, 68
Prenatal Essence, 11
Prenatal Fire, 44
Prenatal Qi, 68
Pritikin Diet, 29
promiscuity, 63, 67
protein, 23
pulse fine and deep, 45
pulse fine, retarded, hollow, 54
pulse, forceless, 32
pulse, slippery, 41
pulse slow, thready, 39
pulse, sluggish, 71
pulse stronger, fuller, 48
pulse thready, 51
pulse weak, 39
pulse wiry, 32, 42, 46, 48
pumpkin, 41, 42, 60, 62
pungent taste, 19
Qi, 11, 5
Qi, Blood, and Liquid, 11
Qi Deficiency, 49
Qi Deficiency, Blood Deficiency, 32, 51
Radish, 37, 42, 60
raspberry, 37, 68
raw food, 9, 32
raw fruits and vegetables, 52
Rebellious Qi, 11, 43
red meat, 42, 47, 69, 71
reduced sexual performance, 43
rheumatism, 64
rhinorrhea, 54
rhubarb, 48, 62
rice, 62, 64, 68
rice bran syrup, 41
rice congee with carrot, 60
rich foods, 42
Righteous Qi, 36, 59, 62, 67, 77
root vegetables, 14
rosemary, 47, 64
runny nose, 59
rutabaga, 41
Safflower, 47, 53
saffron, 47, 53
salad, 41
salt, 37, 69, 70
salt, excessive consumption, 32, 42, 70
salt, tonifying Kidney Yin, 70
salt, topical applications of, 71
salting foods, 14
salty taste, 19

sardine, 37, 42
scallion, 42, 47, 59
Scarsdale Diet, 29
sciatica, 32, 43
seaweed, 35, 41, 42, 48, 61
sensation of lump in throat, 46
sesame oil, 55
sex, 62, 67, 79
shark meat, 37, 42, 60, 61
shellfish, 42
Shen, 11, 32, 62
shortness of breath, 54
shrimp, 37, 42, 68
sinus headache, 43
Six Evils, 47
Six Qi, 7, 16
Six Stages of Cold Disease, 16
skin eruptions, watery, 41
skin inflammations, 41, 66
skinniness, 54
sneezing, 43, 59
soft rice, 41
sore throat, 59, 60, 61
soreness in knees, 65
soups, 59
sour foods, overconsumption of, 32
sour taste, 19
soy products, 35, 60
soybean, 42
spermatorrhea, 63
spices, 14, 47
spinach, 35, 42
Spleen, 20, 56, 69
Spleen Cold, 45
Spleen, Damp, 42, 65
Spleen Deficiency, 39, 40, 44, 49, 54
Spleen, in blood formation, 51
Spleen, weak, 32
Spleen Yang Deficiency, 39
spots in front of eyes, 45, 51
Spring, 14, 9
Sputum, 43
squash, 35
Stagnant Blood in Lower Burner, 31, 73
Stagnant Blood, 52
Stagnant Qi, 11
Stagnation of Qi and Blood, 8
Stirring of Endogenous Liver Wind, 48
Stomach, 56, 69
Stomach Fire, 13
Stomach Hot, 45
Stomach Qi, 12
Stomach/Spleen Deficiency, 39, 42, 43